Flying South
No. 8
2021

Managing Editor:	Steve Lindahl
Poetry Editor:	Mary Hennessy
Non-fiction Editor:	Jennifer Stevenson Vincent
Fiction Editor:	Bob Shar
Fiction Readers:	Ray Morrison
	Steve Lindahl

President's Favorite chosen by:
        Judie Holcomb Pack

Cover Art: Barbara Rizza Mellin

Flying South is a literary magazine/writing contest published annually by Winston-Salem Writers, an association of writers and readers with the purpose of:

Helping writers interact with other writers, improve their craft, and realize their goals.

Information about Winston-Salem Writers can be found at the website: **www.wswriters.org**

Winston-Salem Writers is a non-profit organization and a member of The Arts Council of Winston-Salem and Forsyth County, NC.

Contents

2021 Best in Category Winners:

Fiction:

Non-Fiction:

Poetry:

Julie Means Kane

I Remember You

Back in the days when North Carolina was just waking up to find the twentieth century half gone, a fellow by the name of Robert Henry Taft rose when the first church bells rang out on the other side of the river. He washed in the basin, shaved with care, then brushed down his only suit. He would be attending services with his mother this morning, something he rarely did these days, but he had been given no choice today. When she pulled up to the curb outside, he was waiting for her.

Junior—everybody called him Junior—didn't have much to say on the ride out to the little dirt-road church where he'd grown up singing in the choir. His mother was full of talk about Miz Harris's sister's girl who would be speaking after the service. Junior kept his eyes straight ahead, nodding when she paused for breath. He was trying to prepare himself for the folks he would be seeing and the questions they would have for him. He didn't always know just what to say and mostly kept his eyes down and his voice low. He followed his mother across the grass and up to the church door, and it wasn't until he heard Miz Harris call his name that he looked up.

"Junior, this is my niece Jolanda from Chicago, Illinois. Jolanda, meet Junior Taft."

Junior opened his mouth to say hello, but his jaw just hung there. The woman from Chicago didn't miss a beat. "So glad to see you, Junior," and she turned to the next couple, smiling and extending her hand.

"Come on, boy, let's get inside," said his mother as she pulled him away.

Just before the service began, Miz Harris and Jolanda walked up the aisle to their seats on the front row. Junior raised his eyes enough to see the sway of Jolanda's hem then went back to studying his knuckles. The choir came in, their shoes echoing on the bare floorboards, and when they went to singing, the dust just flew down from the rafters. His mother shifted forward in her seat, swaying with the rhythm of clapping hands, but Junior was far away in a west-side corner bar in Memphis where the dust rose up from the floor when the band hit its groove. He'd washed glasses and swept the place out in exchange for a bed in the back and a chance to play and sing a little on slow nights. On the weekends, he would be found sitting alone at a back table, nursing a beer and watching the crowd. He held on there for four years, keeping his head down and saving up the dimes and quarters he collected in his tip jar until he had enough for a bus ticket back home.

Junior looked up when the preacher called on Sister Alston to read the lesson. A shaft of sunlight from the open window fell full across her face as she started reading, and Junior was reminded of another face lit by a stray beam of light in that dark and throbbing bar years ago. It had been past midnight, the music tight and the dancers feeling it when he'd caught sight of a woman, a beautiful woman, with half-closed eyes, moving with the heavy bass beat, lost in the moment. He'd watched her through the swirling smoke, and then she'd been taken up by the dancers, absorbed, gone.

The choir stood and began to sing. With the dragging beat of "I Know I Been Changed" insinuating its way through the congregation, bodies began to sway until one by one men and women rose from their seats, stretching out to heaven. Beside Junior, his mother whispered "Thank you, Jesus, thank you," and in the front row, Miz Harris was on her feet and moving with the Spirit while Jolanda sat with her head back and eyes closed. Junior's head was down, but the fingers on his left hand moved through the familiar chords with the choir. When the tambourines came out, he looked up to see the singers' white collars shining through the dusty air and the flash of fire when the ringing cymbals caught the light.

She'd worn a red dress, he remembered, and some high heeled shoes. He couldn't understand what a woman like that was doing way down on the wrong side of Memphis, but Junior was smart enough not to question some things. The preacher was back up in the front of the church now, doing the holy dance and getting ready to preach. As the choir finished, he took his spot by the old piano and laid his open Bible down, stroking his hand down the smooth pages to hold them in place. He pulled a handkerchief from his pocket and placed it beside the Book. And then he started in.

Miracles come along at the strangest times in the strangest places, and it was at the bar that this one had happened. Junior had gone up intending to quench his thirst, and there she was. Somehow, he'd found his voice. "Buy you a drink?"

She'd tilted her head and gave him a cool look. "I'll have a margarita. No salt."

He'd had a beer.

They danced until the lights came up at 2 am, then they walked down the block to an all-night diner. She hadn't said much about herself, just wanted to know about Junior. She'd been quiet when he pulled a creased photo out of his pocket and told her how it was, coming up with a father who was a hustler and a stranger to him. It was something he'd never told anybody, about how he never knew why his daddy left him or what he might look like today. They drank their coffee, then she got up, gave him a long kiss and walked out the door. It tore his heart apart.

The preacher was starting to whoop, and the congregation had gone to shouting and reaching. His mother was on her feet, her right arm in the air. The tambourines were banging with the rhythm of the preaching, and all around the room, the ladies were fanning themselves. Miz Harris had kicked off her shoes and was starting to shout, but Jolanda sat, moving a little in time with the calls around her. No one but the Lord heard Junior say, "Thank you, Jesus."

After the service, Jolanda went up to stand by the piano and speak about her work as a civil rights lawyer on the discrimination cases that were beginning to stack up in courtrooms around the country. Junior sat quietly while the other members of the congregation murmured their approval or called out, "Amen!" or "You tell it, sister!" Miz Harris beamed, looking around at her friends and nodding. Leaning forward with his hands between his knees, Junior studied Jolanda's face, then with a nod he sat back again.

Now, in this part of the country, no speaker would be allowed to go on her way without being fed and fed well. Outside the church, the ladies were putting their final touches to dinner on the ground. Junior walked over to the group of folks standing in the shade of a big old oak tree, talking to Jolanda. He stood there quietly as, one by one, the others moved away until it was just the two of them.

"Do I look familiar," he asked, "in any kind of way?"

Before Jolanda could respond, Sister Alston called out, "Everybody, y'all come on over here so Pastor can bless this food."

Fried chicken, ham biscuits, butter beans, slaw, field peas, okra, cocoanut pie – these ladies knew how to fill a person's belly. Miz Taft led her son over to a table where they were joined by Miz Harris and Jolanda. After just a minute, the pastor and Sister Alston sat down with them, and the talk was about Dr. Martin Luther King Jr. down in Atlanta and the lunch counter sit-in over in Greensboro.

Pastor was saying how Dr. King was a man of God and how it was right to meet anger with peaceful determination, and Sister Alston was nodding right along with him, when Miz Taft looked like she was about to choke on her fork full of pie.

"You just stop that talk right there," she said from behind her napkin. "All these ideas might be fine for them that lives up north, but we've got to get along with folks around here, and it's not been that long since the last cross was burned in this county. We don't need any churches burned or our young men going missing."

Miz Harris colored up and just turned her head away while Sister Alston whispered something to Junior's mother. Jolanda opened her mouth to speak but closed it when she saw Pastor's frown. She turned to Junior and met his eyes, but he looked down at his plate. He just didn't know what to say, but once or twice when he looked up, he thought he saw Jolanda still looking his way.

When the older women went off with the pastor to get their coffee, Jolanda looked him full in the face.

"What did you say to me over there before we started to eat?"

"I asked you did I look familiar."

"Should you?"

"You don't remember me, but I remember you."

"I was wearing a red dress, and you had a worn-out old picture of your daddy. Yes, I remember you."

Junior waved away a fly. As was usual with him, he couldn't think what to say.

"You didn't stay in Memphis?" she asked.

"Naw. What were *you* doing down there?"

"I was at a conference. It was just all so serious, and I went looking for some music."

"Well, you sure gave Junior a night he'd never forget."

Jolanda touched his hand, and Junior drew a steadying breath. Just then a car rolled onto the grass, and at the sound of its horn, Jolanda drew back her hand. It was an air-conditioned Oldsmobile, baby blue with white sidewalls. The driver, a light-skinned man in a sports coat and tie, stepped out and waved at Jolanda.

"You ready, girl?"

"Just about," she answered as the driver ambled over to join them. "Junior, this is Thomas Massengail. He works for the NAACP."

Now, in those days in a small country church outside a small North Carolina town, saying a person worked for the NAACP was like saying here's Moses, ready to lead you to the Promised Land. What could Junior have to say that would interest a man like this? So he just stood there, not making a sound while Jolanda went off to say goodbye to her aunt. Both men followed her with their eyes.

"You live around here?" Massengail finally asked with a look a Junior's suit and shoes.

"It's not so bad," Junior mumbled without taking his gaze off Jolanda as she shook the pastor's hand.

"What do you people do when you're not in church?" His vowels told Junior the man had been raised up north. Junior had never been north of Richmond.

"Farm, mostly. I work in a mill." He would have liked to be anywhere but where he was. He lowered his eyes to the ground, where he picked out a team of ants wrestling a piece of biscuit through the grass at his feet. Junior could identify.

"God! 'Tote that barge, lift that bale!' It could still be 1910 down here." Massengail took out a white handkerchief and carefully applied it to his forehead and upper lip. "Sure is hot." He turned away and called to Jolanda, "We better get on the road, girl. It's an hour to Raleigh."

She passed Junior on the way to the car, and whispered, "Got to go." He couldn't look her in the eye, standing there in his one suit and second-hand tie.

The car pulled off, its tires spitting gravel as it hit the dirt road. Junior found his mother and pulled her away from her friends, saying "Let's go. I need to get out of these clothes. Don't know why I came out here today anyway."

Later that week, with the August sun beating down and not a breath of air moving, Junior walked across the river, hands in his pockets, to the post office. The streets were almost empty with most folks having enough sense to spend the afternoon on a shady front porch or in a living room with drawn curtains and an oscillating fan. As Junior climbed the hill from the bridge, he could hear his pulse in his ears and feel the sweat soaking into the neck of his shirt. He was parched, but he passed the court house with its two water fountains out front. He would be damned if he would drink from the one labeled "Colored." For a nickel, he could buy a fountain Coke from Pleasant's Drug Store and drink it at the curb.

As he passed, he slowed his pace to get a better look at the little group coming down the court house steps. He could see several men he recognized as leaders of the local Negro community and in their midst a woman in a dark suit. As they reached the sidewalk, the men spread out and Junior recognized Jolanda there, in serious conversation with her companions. Someone passed a remark, and she laughed, then shook hands all around, and the group broke apart. She was heading on over toward a bench in the shade, and that's when Junior noticed that Massengail character waiting there.

Junior turned away and kept on walking, but Jolanda had seen him now and was headed in his direction with Massengail in tow. She called out to him, and Junior stopped and turned. There was no way to avoid this meeting. He glanced down at his old blue shirt and wished he had taken time after work to change his clothes.

"Junior! I was hoping I'd run into you again. I just got a look at the court house and met Judge Harris. I'd say he's not as bad as some I've come across down here."

Junior couldn't help but smile at her enthusiasm. Here was a woman who threw her whole self into whatever she was doing. It was easy to be carried along with her.

"I was just going to get me a fountain Coke at that drug store across the street. Can I get you one, too?"

"I'd like that."

The other man looked Junior up and down, then said, "Don't worry about me, I'm not thirsty."

When Junior returned with the two cups of soda, he found Jolanda on a bench with Massengail leaning over her shoulder. As Jolanda took a sip of her drink, Massengail stood up and said, "I know we've got work to do down here, but it seems to me that folks around this town don't care much about improving things for themselves or their children."

Junior kicked hard at a pebble, and Jolanda looked up with a frown.

"I mean, half the people I talk to say they're doing all right, and the other half say, don't rock the boat. Meanwhile, they go right on farming the white man's land for him, then paying too much for groceries in his store. I've got to get back up north. I've had about all the chitlin's and turnip greens I can take." And he turned his back and walked away.

"Well," said Jolanda. Junior was studying the toe of his shoe.

"Come sit down," she said, "and tell me what you've been doing since you left Memphis. Still playing guitar?"

Junior sat down and took a deep breath. He was not a man who expected to make much of an impression, and he was surprised that she remembered this detail from their conversation years before. He gave her the short version of his story, coming back home to find a mill job – better than following the backside of a mule – and a room in town. He told her about playing and singing on weekends at a barrel house by the river and said, no, he didn't miss Memphis much.

While he spoke, Jolanda watched his eyes, smiling at his small successes and touching his arm when he talked about his father who was still among the missing. He was just beginning to wonder how he had so much to say when Massengail walked up, checking his watch, then stopping in front of the bench.

"Come on, Jolanda, I want to get back to Raleigh in time to shower before dinner."

"We've got plenty of time, Thomas," she said and turned back to Junior. She was telling him about her work with South Side parents, helping them challenge the policies of the Chicago School Board. Junior was impressed. This was way beyond anything in his experience, and he wanted to hear more.

Massengail loosened his tie and paced over to the fountains and back, stopping periodically to pull back his starched cuff and glare at his watch. Jolanda ignored him. She and Junior had finished their drinks and their shadows were stretching out across the sidewalk, but they still had more to say to each other. Anyone passing would think they were old friends.

"Damn, girl. How much more time are you going to waste with Buckwheat here? I don't know about you, but I've got better things to do."

Jolanda turned to look at Massengail's angry face, then looked back at Junior. Neither spoke.

"Why not just finish up here with your life story and say goodbye to the nice lady, JUN-i-or?"

8 *Julie Means Kane*

Now, the thing to know about Junior is that he was not a violent man. He was big enough to appear threatening if he had wanted to, but that had never been his way. He was a patient man and had learned that most problems sorted themselves out with a little time. Now, when he stole a look at Jolanda's shocked expression, he felt a tightening in his gut.

Slowly, thoughtfully, he rose to his feet. He didn't want to get this wrong.

"What did you say, *Mister* Massengail?" he asked in a low voice. For once, he looked the man straight in the eye.

"I said, say goodbye to the lady and get on your way, *Jun*-ior."

Without taking a beat, Junior's arm came up to deliver a left hook that caught Massengail on the jaw. He took a step back and looked down at the man who was now on one knee, shaking his head and rubbing the side of his face.

"My name is Robert Henry Taft," he said. "You can call me Mr. Taft. Maybe you can even call me Robert. But *don't* call me Junior."

He reached out a hand to help Massengail to his feet, then turned to Jolanda.

"You okay?" he asked while he rubbed his knuckles.

She raised an eyebrow in his direction, then with a small nod, she took Massengail's arm and led him off toward his car, leaving Junior standing on the sidewalk. He watched them walk away, but just before they rounded the corner, he saw Jolanda look back and smile. He stood up a little straighter and waved.

It would be nice to think that Robert Taft and Jolanda married and lived a long and fruitful life. Things don't often work that way, though, and in truth they never met again. Robert, never Junior now, kept on working at the mill and got his satisfaction from his music, playing and singing on Saturday nights, then doing the same thing in church on Sunday mornings. After a year or two, he married Sister Alston's girl, and people say they were as happy as most folks. When they had their first boy, they named him after his father, but they always called him Bobby.

Zachariah Claypole White

The Coup
(Language is a Violence to Rise with the Sea)

November 10, 1898
Alex Manly's press will burn

in flame-kissed photos
white supremacists pose
an orchestra awaiting its curtain fall

men stand beneath the dangling sky
grind heels into half-printed headlines
hold nooses like cello strings

state militia are dispatched
only black citizens are arrested

local newspapers
led by the Raleigh-based
News and Observer
help instigate the overthrow
swallow the ash of darker words

each day the *News and Observer*
arrives under my window

I skim pages
tear them into cardinal wings
taste another's blood in the ink

reach for violence
       the smoke under my fingertips

my brother says
    muzzled words

are feral things
clawing at our lips

i say *yes*

we understand

+++

November 1898
Wilmington executes
sixty or more black citizens
hands like mine
do not record
the exact number

sometimes i leave the word *history* in my coat pocket
hand it to a gas station attendant
neither of us sure
how many gallons
it is worth

protests continue
i try to speak with the ghost
sharing my seat
but our tongues have fallen
between the pews

officials note
> *the neighborhood*
> *declined*

decline
      which might be a synonym
      for overthrow
      for no whites arrested
      for lynch

i believe a nation
is a bird with no feet

This poem quotes from:
"Wilmington, North Carolina's Taylor Estates Redevelopment Project." n.d.
      Web. 23 Apr. 2017.

Carolyn Willis

The Green Dress

I tell you there was a green dress many years ago in a shop near the bay; sage green, that dusky green, like the underside of schefflera leaves bunched in close to the trunk way up high on a cloudy day. Just a simple dress, elegant, with small, satin buttons, that I pictured unbuttoned, of course. You know, just a hint of tanned breast and lots of tanned neck.

And when I tried it on, well, all I know is that for a while in that dressing room, I forgot my daughter, I forgot the rent, I forgot we were out of most everything, but more than anything, I forgot the struggle our life had become.

Because when it shimmered down my body, I knew. You know how you know it's gonna be perfect? How it's gonna make *you* perfect, beyond vanity, I mean, like a baptismal robe, drenched in transformation. How it's gonna bring out the beauty of your soul, strengthen, and push your best right through, like that angel inside you spread its wings and shoved you out of its way.

And all those years of denial and sacrifice and worry can bead up and drop right off you, like water off a body dipped down in holy oil as you finally feel free to shake it all off and rise to admire yourself. How for once you're not coming up short and wondering why the world has to bring a woman down so low.

So there I stood, alone in that dressing room with tears running down my cheeks onto all the butter-soft silk that clung and draped and molded me into a different future, one I'd not glimpsed in a long, long time: Me, striding free with yards of green swirling round my hips and legs.

But I knew I couldn't buy it. I knew I wouldn't buy it, because of my daughter's eyes. And because I didn't know then I'd grieve for that dress the rest of my life. And I didn't know then I'd face hard times pretending to wear it, as if I really *was* the owner of a dress like that.

Yet even then I knew that dress was something poor women have missed, something so very important, for there's not enough green dresses in the whole damn world to dry their tears, and that maybe just once, it'd really be fine to sleep unfettered from those all-night-long, desperate thoughts.

And, yeah, I could have faced God in that dress, because in it, I was so simply a Goddess.

Angela Maere

Wonder If They Love Each Other

April 24, 2021
Paris, France

Nearing the end of the 3rd Lockdown for COVID-19 (curfew: 6pm, changed two weeks ago to 7pm due to daylight savings)

Wonder if they love each other. These couples in the apartment windows I peer into against my best attempts and better judgement. We are neighbors who live face to face who do what we can to avoid looking at each other in the face. A birds-eye view into each other's private lives, yet we try not to pry. Wonder if they love each other.

The ones on the sixth floor are busy catching their bouncy curly haired daughter, a tot who only recently discovered her legs can run—whether she's running into dad's open arms, or running from her parent's attempts to corral her onto the couch for bedtime story…oh bedtime story. Mom and dad love that. It's que that they are commencing their daily reprieve from the never-ending role that is parenthood. After 8pm, they get to no longer act as a playmate and food dispenser and return to the adult world in which they feel a bit more human—more themselves. Mom in particular loves bedtime story. She sinks into the couch as if waiting for it to swallow her whole, and spit her back up as a new, improved, and shinier version of herself. Mom 2.0. Dad doesn't mind taking over bedtime story from time to time, but it seems to be mom's "thing." It is, however, never a thing they do together. They do come together on that same couch to talk over a late-night snack, watch a film while having a cuddle, and, lately, to have a few arguments. Then dad gets up off the couch and walks away. He instead sits at the dining room table behind mom, obliviously scouring the internet on his laptop as she patters about on her cellphone, frustratedly texting a confidant who *will* listen to her, about how *he* doesn't listen to her. And that is the end of that "thing" for the night. Wonder if they love each other.

One floor and a 20-year age gap above the young parents, sits the art lovers who love looking after their outdoor shrubbery as much as they love an evening bottle of rouge. Wonder if they love each other. They have more time on their hands since there are no little hands waving at them, feverishly vying for their attention. The reoccurring visit of a twenty-something who has the same nose as the woman of the house implies that this was not always the case. They share afternoon tea and laugh adoringly at the photo that didn't turn out right when she wanted to capture a memory of the moment with the sun gleaming into sunset. Wonder if they love each other. Around 8:30pm, man and wife sit down together for dinner in their sitting room, adorned with artwork that is tactfully hung on the walls. A grand piece taking center focus. Black brush strokes on a white canvas, it appears as a psychological que card— what do you *really* see here? She reads a lot. Appreciates culture and education, generally preferring to keep things in order. He has more unkept tastes-watering plants that need trimming and occasionally breaking the unspoken neighborly rule of not staring--or at least, not getting caught doing so. I look up to see him looking over. He looks away, a bit embarrassed if our eyes meet. I find myself feeling generally alright with it. It does not happen an overwhelming amount and, like me, it appears the glances are merely a natural and somewhat impulsive curiosity regarding other human beings, rather than wandering eyes with an intention to stray. Though sometimes, I sense he's spending more time on the patio watering his plants than necessary. Perhaps he feels guilty. To spare himself the inner dialogue of shame, he's made note of the curious creature living across the way to his wife. Now they both look at me through their window and into mine from time to time. Sometimes together over dinner. Observing, or keeping a wary eye on me, who's to say? I am not one to judge. I continue my curious mannerisms, dancing about with my pet rabbit in my arms or typing madly away on my laptop into odd hours of the morning. To them I say, let your patio foliage bloom like your love. Wonder if they love each other. Wonder if that's why he's never trimmed the hedges. A never-ending growth of endearment.

After each sunset the night settles in on my coupled-up neighbors just as it settles in around me. The deep shades of enveloping blues and black have crept in and erased the daylight. I look back through the window and another character now appears. Quite recognizable, and curious indeed. Staring back at myself, I wonder...

Wonder if someday I will have someone who makes me laugh in the glimmering sun, whom I argue with, whom I share a bottle of wine and a film with, who frustrates me, whom I eat dinner with every night, who shares their inner dialogue with me and I with them, and years of our lives together. Someone who, when we're observed together from a distance, makes others think, "wonder if they love each other."

Bob Wickless

Perfect Light

Sometimes I believe
In the last light, at nearly dusk,
And I want to call it
Perfect light, the only light
In which everything understands
What it truly is
Without shadow, without glare,
In a single, defining moment,
The same light
By which an exquisite canvas,
Illuminated from within,
Renders the well-known
Into forever.

Sometimes called the gloam—
A term now chiefly poetic—
As *I saw their starved lips in the gloam*,
When poor Keats, dreaming the dead,
Is summoned by
La Belle Dame Sans Merci.
A time, too, when no birds sing
But engage in flat, tentative flights
As if they are entering water
They don't fully trust
And skim off the summer grass
Like stones shallow skipped
By a sidearm spinning toss—
Hence the strong, invisible arm
Of God.

Now I ask you this:
Why is it always dusk,
The figurative bottom of the ninth,
When God, old ace in relief,
Appears on the mound
To wrap up someone else's series?
Is it to allow us this instant,
This glimpse of Godly perfection,
Or is it to serve up the perfect sinker
And shut daylight out
While the diamond, the whole field darkens,
And the crowd settles into a hush,
Knowing something has been stolen,
Something returned in the loss,
And something, surely there must
Have been something else won—
But they can't quite catch it,
That flying perfection,
No matter how they maneuver,
How they position their tiny,
Grasping, outstretched arms.

Gary Chew

Paradox

Joy is not found on the flipside of sad
Show me a shadow without its object
Paint me a rainbow before a downpour
Shed tears of joy without trials endured

I am a coin spiralling on a table top
Shadow and light; truth and lie
Jazz is alive for it longs to resolve
Poetic beauty lies in our paradox

Leigh Fairchild-Coppoletti

The Magic Box

City Museum was a former shoe factory that had been converted into a kind of three-dimensional Chutes and Ladders board with ten stories of spiraling staircases and snaking slides. More of a small amusement park than a museum, it was indoors and outdoors, a surreal playground for all ages, its exhibits untethered to any single theme: vintage pinball machines, antique door knobs, pinned insects. The sun was beginning to set but still blistering. Lauren and Owen wore shorts and tee shirts, and they sat across from each other in the museum's rooftop cantina. In the distance was the glowing steel of the Arch.

"I've been studying too much," Lauren said. She dipped a tortilla chip in spicy guacamole. "The Arch is reminding me of the inverted U theory that Dr. Atkins talked about."

"Yerkes-Dodson," Owen said. He had freckles, a lean runner's build, coppery locks that were long enough to tie in a topknot. His tee-shirt said, *Burning Kumquat Hootenanny.* "I thought about it when I wanted to ask you out. Because I needed enough nerve to talk to you. But not so much that I'd be all creepy."

She smiled. "That law keeps taking on new meanings for me."

Owen had not needed to ask her out. On the eve of their psychology final, they had found themselves in the same study group. It was in Owen's apartment, and he had made teriyaki stir fry with vegetables harvested from Burning Kumquat, the campus gardens. At the end of the study session, he handed her a paper bag of fresh herbs. Rosemary, cilantro, thyme. In the week since then, they had explored the book stores and restaurants on Cherokee Street, listened to jazz in Holmes Hall, and discussed the oxymoron of clean coal and the eco-potential of fungi. These were all things Lauren had not made time to do in her first year of college.

She ran her fingers through her bangs, which were damp and sticking to her forehead. "Yerkes-Dodson reminds me of my dad. He's a master at being in the optimal zone. By mustering just the right amount of motivation to do what he needs to do."

"I have a new goal," Owen said, his eyes brightening. "Being dubbed a master of the optimal zone."

They had both ordered orange pop, and the bottles were beaded with sweat. "Stress makes things impossible for me," she said. "I'm not wired for it."

"You were so focused in class. I could never get you to make eye contact. Don't you get stressed about school?"

"Not if I plan ahead."

"Another Dr. Atkins gem--studies show we're happier when we're planning ahead," he said, waving his forefinger, imitating their professor. "It's what makes us different from other animals."

She laughed, thinking of Dr. Atkins, her frizzy hair and tortoiseshell glasses. "But over-planning can make it hard to follow our guts."

He loaded a chip with guacamole. "I want to be more gutsy about travel. Really immerse myself in places and not just be a tourist."

"I always feel like a tourist. Wherever I am." This last comment surprised her, the kind of elusive nugget of self-understanding that took shape from the elements of conversation. "Maybe because I'm sensitive about other people's expectations. It's an adopted kid thing. Always trying to prove that I fit in."

"Your parents probably expect a lot," he said. "With you and your sisters being Chinese."

She took a chip and broke it in half. "They have high expectations," she said, putting the chips on her plate. "Which aren't related to where I was born."

"I only meant it as a compliment."

"My parents just wanted children."

"It's cool they encouraged you to learn Chinese."

She picked up the moist pop bottle, took a sip. "They've always talked about me going to China to visit," she said. "I grew up watching Chinese Central Television. CCTV-4."

"ESPN played nonstop at my house, mostly basketball. I like playing sports but not really watching them. Fishing's my favorite."

"It goes well with gardening." She looked at the Arch, the hazy amber sky. "Both have to do with what I want to do in China one day. Studying the role of nature in daily spiritual life."

"My parents don't get my love for gardening. They spend more time in Costco than outdoors."

"My parents have evolved," she said. "I wanted to do more about environmental protection at our church. Their church. And they got me a Bible with the nuttiest, crunchiest passages highlighted in green."

"I'm surprised you're going on a cruise," he said. "Those ships definitely don't compost."

"It was a surprise at Christmas," she said. "I didn't want to hurt their feelings. And I'm hoping it will be a good time to tell them how I feel about church. How I'm not going back."

"Could put a damper on the vacation."

"Maybe I'll wait. Tell them after."

"What will they say about you going out with a non-church guy?"

She looked at his eyes, the blue warmth of them. *Going out.* "I'm sure they will come around."

He finished his pop. "Don't back down. Some stress is necessary for optimal performance."

She smiled. "From now on, that's what the Arch is going to symbolize for me."

They slid down one of the steep former shoe chutes to a complicated network of plaster caves, and they navigated the nooks and tunnels, eventually settling into a dimly lit alcove with enough room for them to sit side by side. They could see into a larger area of steps and paths with walls carved into the shape of sharp-toothed scaly dragons. Small groups and couples meandered occasionally past them.

"I love the 'seagrass' hanging from the ceiling in the lobby," Lauren said.

"It's made from strips of Boeing parachute silk," Owen said. "I can't believe you haven't been here. It's perfect for you, a laboratory for sustainability. Nothing's wasted."

Owen's kneecaps were as freckled as his cheeks, the hair on them translucent. She put her hand on one knee, slid it up his thigh. He kissed her, and she smelled musk, tasted the sweet residue of orange pop on his lips.

"I could go to China with you," he said, his face just an inch from hers, his hands holding hers.

"We could explore Chinese gardens," she said. "Then design our own spiritual landscapes."

"Spirit-scapes."

"Escapes from the emptiness of things."

He tightened his hands around hers. "We could bring the project to New Mexico."

"Maybe even after the cruise," she said, "I could visit you in Albuquerque. We could hike in the Sandias." Owen's eyes had lit up when he first told her about the mountains, about how Sandia means watermelon in Spanish, how the mountains turned watermelon pink at sunset. She had imagined hiking on the mountain trails with Owen, talking about psychology.

"You'll need to tell your parents about church, though," he said. "So they'll be more likely to accept me."

"It's got to be the right time."

"What if there never seems to be a right time, Lauren?"

"My parents know me pretty well," she said. "They probably have a sense that I'm not going back to their church anyway."

"Maybe they don't." He let go of her hands. "And you said you try to avoid stress."

She looked at the floor below them tiled with blue mosaics, at a dragon's head with eyes the size of grapefruits. "I said I planned to talk to them."

"Don't be defensive," he said. "There's just reason for concern."

"What reason?"

He brushed his hair back with his hands. "It's okay. Never mind."

"Tell me," she said.

"I don't want it to sound wrong." He rested his head against the wall. "Some girls, I think a lot of Asian girls, have a harder time with confrontation. Throw a background of evangelicalism in there and…."

She looked at him, waiting until he turned to her. "That's so stereotypical, Owen."

"See, you're upset," he said. "This is why I didn't want to say anything."

She scooted out of the alcove, stood.

He followed her, took her hands. "It's a concern, Lauren," he said. "*Because* I want things to work between us."

"I appreciate that," she said.

They took an Uber back to the university, and Owen apologized again. When he kissed her goodnight, she turned her head, and his kiss landed on her cheek.

***

The Diamond Navigator had docked in Tortola, Puerto Rico, and St. Maarten, and their time onboard had been pleasant--backgammon by the pool, lavish meals, and lectures about the pirates of the Virgin Islands. Blackbeard, Captain Kidd, Anne Bonny. Her father had taken to saying "aar" instead of "yes." Her mother and Grace learned how to fold cloth napkins into swans on the quarterdeck, and Lauren and Molly read on lounge chairs. Grace and Molly were twins, 14 years old and identical.

In Havana, they exchanged dollars for a special Cuban currency for foreigners, the CUC, a convertible currency equal to one U.S. dollar and worth far more than a Cuban peso, the CUP. They explored the cobblestone streets of the old city with a guide who said he was also an engineer. He brought them to El Floridita, a crowded tourist restaurant that Ernest Hemingway frequented and that featured a lifesize bronze statue of Hemingway at the bar. Grace, who kept her long hair in a ponytail, flipped through *Lonely Planet Cuba*, and Molly looked out the window, which faced a row of three-wheel yellow buggies, waiting for customers, their curved cabs resembling coconut halves. Coco-taxis. Lauren's parents ordered *ropa vieja*, a shredded beef dish with spearmint and onions, and pop for everyone. Lauren asked for a strawberry daiquiri.

"I guess this is the place to have one," her mother said. She disapproved of drinking, but Lauren had drunk wine once with her dinner on the ship, and her mother's begrudging acceptance made Lauren more confident about moving beyond other tensions. This had not happened with Owen. She had felt self-conscious around him, feeling pressure to prove her gumption, and since he had left for New Mexico in July, she had not responded to his calls or texts.

"The cars from the fifties," Lauren said. "They remind me of this museum in St. Louis. Where everything's reused. All of Havana is like this museum."

"I don't think you're wrong to want less waste, Lauren," her father said. "But Cubans are reusing things because they have no other choice."

"We did research," her mother said. "Cubans can't even have beef. Only tourists. After the Soviets left, many people starved. They…" Her mother leaned over the table. "They ate their cats."

"Gross," Grace said.

"We want you girls to understand the consequences of socialism," her father said.

The waiter brought their drinks, and Lauren sipped her daiquiri. "Is this about me supporting Bernie?"

"I felt the Bern too," Molly said. She had recently cut her hair, chin-length, and it made her look a year or two older than Grace.

"Which is why we looked for an itinerary that included Cuba," her father said.

"I didn't want to come here," her mother said. "We're giving good money to a corrupt regime."

"I don't get it," Lauren said. "It's not like I'd ever support totalitarianism."

"But that's where socialism leads, Lauren," her father said.

"Sanders is a *democratic* socialist," Lauren said.

"He wants to lift up the poor," Molly said. "Like Jesus."

"More like Che," her father said.

"Who overthrew a tyrant and then helped install a new tyrant," her mother said, speaking fast. "Then ordered the execution of all counter-revolutionaries without trial and got rid of the free press."

Lauren drew her fingers down the margarita glass, collapsing the tiny pearls of condensation, imagining her parents rehearsing this moment, planning for it. "I don't even know what I'd call myself politically," she said. "I think I'm looking for something that doesn't exist yet. And anyway, there's a huge difference between the revolutionary socialism of Che and Bernie Sanders."

"It's a slippery slope," her father said.

"At least there's a lot of diversity here," Molly said.

"Come on, Mol," her father said. "All the top leaders are white. Even all the waiters in this restaurant."

"They're also all men," Grace said.

"Let's talk about something else now," her mother said. "Like the ice cream place we'll go to after this."

"I thought they didn't have milk here," Molly said.

"Apparently Fidel Castro loved ice cream," her mother said. "That's what most of the island's milk is used for."

"The only silver lining to the Castro regime," her father said.

"Maybe we should go to a museum," Lauren said. "I'm interested in Santeria."

"La Coppelia is at the top of all the 'things not to miss' lists," her mother said.

The tourists at the bar posed with the Hemingway statue, taking selfies.

***

They took a 1952 pink Chevy taxi along the Malecon to La Coppelia. At least a hundred people were waiting in line.

"That can't be a line for ice cream," Molly said.

Lauren wiped the dampness on her cheekbones with her fingertips, unstuck her bangs from her forehead. The air was briny and thick with exhaust. The line led to a concrete flying saucer-shaped building in the middle of a wooded park.

"The ship has a sundae buffet," Grace said. "Fifteen flavors, a zillion toppings."

A guard in a starched shirt and tan tie stood by a nearby gate. He beckoned to them. "CUC?" he asked.

Her father took out a CUC bill, but the guard did not need proof and ushered them through the gate, pointing in the opposite direction of the spacecraft building to a bright blue cement wall that also said Coppelia in red letters. Beyond it was a white plastic roof, an open air sitting area, and a shed-like building with a large front window and half a dozen customers. Tourists. The spaceship building was for locals.

"I feel like we're cheating," Lauren said.

"But we're paying heaps more," her mother said. "Supporting you know what."

"It's too hot here," Grace said.

They passed a banyan tree with a multitude of roots, some of which were aerial and dangled like rope and others that had met the earth and taken root themselves and thickened into slender trunks. Roots taking root. They filtered the sunlight like vertical blinds, casting parallel bars of shadow onto the paved gray path. A woman, older than her parents, was sitting on the curb near the blue wall. She stood. She wore a long skirt, held out a wooden block the size of a box for kitchen matches.

"You try," the woman said, looking at Lauren. "Open."

Lauren took the block, which looked solid, and she turned it over. Nothing indicated it could open, no hinge or seam, and she began pulling and pushing on the sides and corners. The woman crossed her arms, nodded. Lauren passed the box to her father, and he did the same without any more success.

"Es una caja mágica." The woman took the box, put her fingers on two diagonal corners of one side, and pulled out a drawer-like component. She returned the box to Lauren, who did what the woman had done. Lauren opened it.

"Five dollars," the woman said.

"Me gusta," Lauren said, but she returned the box.

"You like," the woman said. "You buy."

"Let's go," her father said. Her mother and the twins were already at the service window.

"You have one dollar?" the woman asked. "No soap I have. No food for children."

Lauren's dollars were hidden in a compartment of her shoulder bag, but she had a CUC coin in her pocket. She gave this to the woman, who mumbled something, a complaint or insult. She returned to the curb.

They went to the window, waiting just a minute for their turn. There were three flavors. The vendor topped their scoops with a sprinkling of cookie crumbs and a drizzle of caramel, and they brought them to a picnic table under the plastic roof. She and her father sat across from each other and by a thick tree with above ground roots that sprawled from the trunk base like tendons around a bone. Her mother sat next to her, and the twins next to her father.

"I should have bought the box," Lauren said.

"Your dollars wouldn't amount to a drop in a bucket," her father said. "This place needs capitalism."

Lauren guessed her parents had planned all along to discuss economics over Cuban ice cream. Discussion, part two. "They *have* capitalism," Lauren said. "People can make money off tourists. I read that lawyers and doctors make something like $30 a month. But rickshaw pedalers make a lot more. And drivers. With the two currencies, the locals are second class citizens to tourists."

"At least the go-getters have a chance this way," her father said.

Molly wiped her mouth with the back of her hand. "But it's like Apartheid. We just studied that in Global History II."

Two emaciated cats slinked around the table legs. Molly and Grace were trying each other's ice cream, strawberry and chocolate respectively.

"My point is that a lack of capitalism isn't the problem," Lauren said. "The problem is the lack of democracy. Just like in China."

Ice cream dripped down the side of her cone, onto her hand. There were no napkins, and her mother passed her a tissue, rummaged in her purse for more.

"Which is why you'll be spreading the word in China," her father said. "Not politics."

"Spreading the word?" Lauren's pulse raced. "I wasn't planning on that."

Her mother looked up, hand still in her purse. "Why else would you go to China, Lauren?"

"We've been preparing you," he father said. "To share what you've had the privilege to grow up understanding."

"I thought we were talking about a basic roots trip," Lauren said, feeling the dual onset of a headache and stomachache.

"Me too," Molly said, her elbow on the *Lonely Planet*. "I thought you wanted us to practice our Chinese."

"Yes, you should do that," her mother said. "Practice it *in your mission work*."

"I never agreed to do mission work," Lauren said. The tissue was sticky, chocolate-stained. She felt dizzy. Her breaths became shallow. She could not make any more plans about when to discuss her plans: the moment had presented itself. "I'm not planning on doing that in China."

Her father pushed back his chair, stood up and paced. The twins looked at their ice cream. Lauren's head throbbed.

"The Chinese are desperate for salvation," her mother said. "A billion people denied access to His teachings."

Lauren recalled all the documentaries they had watched as a family about missionary work, the lessons on evangelism. She looked at Molly and Grace. "This is why you adopted us. To train us. To turn us into converters of our heathen birth nation."

"Don't include *us* in your meltdown," Grace said.

"Don't include me in your *us*, Grace," Molly said.

Lauren followed her father, who did not usually pace, and she wondered if his talent for being in an optimal performance zone might depend on a kind of family balancing act, if what seemed like mastery was more of a perch between his wife's anxiety and his daughters' eagerness to please him.

"It's not like we have some agenda," her mother said. "We're a family. We went to the Grand Canyon, Disney World. We do family portraits every year."

"But you want us to proselytize," Lauren said.

"To help people, Lauren," her mother said.

Strawberry ice cream trickled down Molly's hand. "There's nothing wrong with them wanting us to do God's work, Lauren."

Lauren stood and tossed the rest of her cone in the garbage. She wiped her hand on her shorts. "I think we have different ideas about God's work."

Her father stopped, faced her. "We'll see what the pastor says when we get home."

"I'm not interested in what the pastor says," Lauren said.

"We're going back to the ship," her father said. "Now."

"I need time alone," Lauren said, her tone measured, her headache diminished.

"You're not going anywhere by yourself on this island," her father said. He gripped her upper arm.

"You're ruining everything, Lauren," Grace said.

Lauren pulled her arm away. "I'll meet you later."

"Your phone doesn't work here," her mother said. "You can't even get directions."

Molly had tears in her eyes. She handed the *Lonely Planet* to Lauren. "There are maps in it."

Lauren took the sticky book, hugged Molly quickly.

She walked away. "The ship will leave without you," her father called after her. "If you're not back by 5:30."

When Lauren came to the banyan, she reached out and dragged her fingers across the smooth bark of its twisting and sinuous trunk, the one trunk comprising many trunks. The woman in the long skirt was still sitting on the curb, her face hardened, her eyes on the ground. Lauren gave her five dollars, and the woman gave her the box.

***

The sky was watery blue with tendrils of cloud, and the facades of the buildings were the colors of mango and guava skin and plantains. In the center of the cobblestone plaza, children ran around a fountain. A man squeezed a corkscrew of churro batter into a vat of bubbling oil.

She sat at a table in an outdoor cafe near the harbor, feeling parched and famished after having walked for almost an hour from Coppelia, the travel guide on the seat next to her. She finished the agua con gas, ordered another and scrambled eggs, and she finished them quickly. Across the plaza, two women strummed guitars, six-stringed and twelve-stringed.

"Laojia," someone said. A man's voice. Mandarin.

Lauren looked up. "Excuse me?" she asked. The man stood only a foot away from her. He had curly black hair, ginger skin. He looked to be in his early twenties.

"You speak English?" He put a slip of paper on the table with the information. "My mother has rooms. You rent one if you need it."

"I'm all set," she said. "You speak Mandarin?"

"My great grandfather is Chinese."

She looked more closely at his eyes, the shallow crease of the lids that tapered toward his nose. "Is there a Chinese population here?" she asked.

"A long time ago. When they need cheap labor, coolies. But now we say we have *el barrio chino* without any *chino*."

"You're here," she said.

"There are many *mestizos*. African, Criollo, Chinese."

"Not working at this restaurant," she said, looking at the pale-skinned waiters moving between the tables.

"Being a waiter is a good job." He looked at her plate. "You have eggs? Most tourists eat meat."

"Do you want to sit down?" she asked.

"I have somewhere to go," he said. "But I wish you a happy vacation." He turned away, took a step, turned back. "Maybe you want to come with me? There is a party."

"My ship leaves in an hour."

"Then there is time."

A waiter was watching her, watching them. She put out more than enough CUC to cover her bill, tucked the room advertisement in her bag. She stood. "I'm Lauren. Lauren Mendenhall."

"Nestor Navarro." He was lean, a head taller than Lauren.

They passed the churro cart, crossed the plaza.

"You work with your mother?" she asked. "Renting rooms."

"Also I study Chinese medicine."

"I want to visit China and not be different-looking."

"I am different everywhere," Nestor said. "My mother is *casi blanca*. Almost white. And I am *salto atrás*."

"*Salto atrás?*"

"The meaning is 'jump back.'"

"I can't stand labels."

"No standing," Nestor said. "Only jumping. Back, forward, over."

She laughed. Their corner of the plaza turned into a narrow street, and in an open doorway, a large family shared a couch and watched television. Lauren remembered the *Lonely Planet*. She had left it at the cafe.

***

Over a bed of coals on the cobblestones of Calle Compostela, Nestor's friends were spit-roasting a pig. Music blared from a balcony, and a dozen people were dancing in the street that was barely wide enough for a car. Smaller children sat on the curb, and two old men sat at a card table, playing dominoes. The men waved and nodded at Nestor. A woman kissed his cheeks, and when Nestor introduced Lauren to her, she kissed Lauren's cheeks, too. All the while, the woman moved to the music, the steady rhythms of percussion and bass.

A man turned onto the street with a cart of enormous avocados, their skin smooth and lime green. "*Aguacates. Aguacates.*"

"Espere," a woman said, her voice coming from above them. Lauren and Nestor looked up. A woman's head was visible above the roof railing.

"That is my Tia Carmen," Nestor said.

"I like the word, esperar," Lauren said. "In English, we see waiting and hoping as separate things."

Carmen tossed a mesh bag over the wall. It was tied to a rope and she lowered it, not far from the smoke of the roasting pig. "Dos, por favor," Carmen said, and the vendor took hold of the bag, scooped out some coins and replaced them with two avocados. Carmen pulled on the rope, hoisted the avocadoes to the roof.

"I hope and wait for you to try a Cuban avocado," Nestor said.

Lauren smiled. "Is that rumba playing?"

"Timba," Nestor said, taking her hands. "A mix of things." He lifted one of her hands, she turned beneath it, and they danced in the coal smoke. When the song finished, they clapped, and the radio host spoke in rapid Spanish. She looked at her watch. It was 5:10.

"You need to go," Nestor said. He pointed to a man in a bicycle rickshaw on the street corner. "That is Tajo. He is very fast."

The sun was still bright, and the moon was visible too, a full moon, its lower half concealed by a cloud. A milky arch. Another song played. Lauren's pulse quickened, but she waved to Tajo and continued to dance with Nestor, thinking about the magic box and how it had seemed so impossible to open.

.

.

Alan Elyshevitz

Bridge and River

That was years ago, the Talmadge Memorial Bridge,
fulcrum into the future. I heard the rasp of its components,
the screech of unbolting beneath my father's wheels.

In a yellow warning zone, large men worked
on reinforcement, the foreman proud of his clipboard,
the engineer distracted by celebrity news.

Down river, islands soaked in an indecisive morning haze.
Just like a child, I imagined metal fatigue, an unlucky collapse
into a gully of hubcaps and condoms, throw rugs and smashed jars of
jam.

My father remained at the wheel, a practitioner of safety,
menial and exacting. His son went nowhere on the algebraic span
of the Talmadge, its ribs without give or forgiveness.

The solicitous river chewed its own banks
when no one was looking. Only a boy,
I had already damaged hundreds of miles of skin.

Now in memory, it's an abstraction, like a bedroom door
missing knob and hinges. A stylized journey should be
therapeutic, not a car key buried in socks and shirts.

The Savannah River is a quarrel with a spouse
postponed, a change in career deferred. It makes
less money and spends minimal time with the kids.

Every night, bare of color, the river goes delirious in the fallacy
of flow. Though a bridge is stout and stationary, I have hauled
the Talmadge five states north, thirty years after they tore it down.

Judith Ferster

The Prodigal
After Israeli elections

You did not welcome me with whole heart,
brother, when I returned
from millennia of wandering.
I had changed, lost
And won wealth many times,
had grown strong in lands
that hated me. You changed at home,
chose a new faith but taught me,
returned twin, to fry felafel
and dance dabke. I grow great
and now you see
that more of our father's house
must be for me. Make room.

Amy Marques

Fragile Things

My grandfather ate like a bird, laughed like a child, and partied from behind the safety of his guitar. I remember him as being quiet. It's not that he didn't speak, but his voice was soft, and he tossed mumbled words over a shoulder as he walked away in midsentence. He didn't stay around to finish his own thought, much less to wait for our reaction.

All of my memories of him are in the big city, but he was raised in the country and farmed for much of his life. Perhaps his restlessness was muscle memory from the endless chores of tending the land and the animals. In the city, he had a tiny workshop where he did the kind of woodwork that might have been beautiful if he had allowed himself time. He never did. His pieces were an amalgam of brilliant creativity and impatient execution. Endearing, but not enduring.

He was a tall man who would have towered over his short wife, but he was so slight that hers was the bigger presence. She spoke for him – and over him, and although he always walked too fast and a few steps ahead, she was usually the one dictating the direction in which to go.

I wonder if it was his emaciated body or the fact that he was in perpetual movement that lent him an air of impermanence. He never really occupied a room. If he sat, it was perched on the edge of the seat, and you wouldn't be wrong to think he might up and leave at any moment.

For as long as I can remember, my grandfather had bad lungs. The first time a *cigarro de palha* touched his lips, he still had baby teeth and although, over half a century later, a son-in-law bullied him into quitting, his lungs were mostly scar tissue by then. He was forever sick, and frequently on the verge of death. The family would gather, all nine children and the countless grandchildren, for another last birthday, last wedding, last visit, or last holiday season with grandpa. But he'd rally. And we'd start the cycle all over again.

My grandmother had always hoped to have a priest and a doctor in the family. I, the second granddaughter, was the first doctor. She is still holding out hope for the priest.

By the time I got into medical school, my grandfather's illness was an unassailable fact of life. The Earth is round, the sky is blue, and *vovô's* lungs were failing, albeit stubbornly functional. I dissected a smoker's lungs in anatomy, studied nicotine damage in physiology, marveled that nobody in the family developed lung cancer from by-proxy smoking, and auscultated the wheezing emphysema in lungs of patients that were not my grandfather.

"You should become a gerontologist," my grandmother said. She didn't need to say the rest, but of course she did. "You could help. You could make things better."

I became a pediatrician. Babies are bundles of potential and parents are full of good intentions. If medicine were a calendar year, pediatrics would be the month of January when all the resolutions for the New Year are still untarnished.

Early in my career, a patient called to say she was in labor. My grandfather was once again in the ICU and I had planned to go see him but decided to delay until after the birth. Babies don't wait, and doctors aren't limited by family visiting hours.

I embraced the parents-to-be, coaxed the newborn into breathing, checked fingers and toes, and showered the new family with accolades. My parting image was of an exhausted mother nursing her newborn while her partner looked on in loving awe.

Few things are as inspiring as ushering a new life into the world. Like fresh notebooks and sunrises, newborns embody limitless possibilities. The elation followed me as I made my way down the gray-green hallways. They look the same to outsiders, but so much of my time was spent in hospitals that I felt at home in the maze of hospital wings.

The light shifts when you walk away from pediatrics and towards the ICU. The walls become grayer and the smells sourer.

I had expected to saunter right in as always. The right kind of name badge and scrubs were a pass into any room. But I was stopped at the door.

The intensivist on shift came to talk to me. His voice was halted and tired. I cannot remember his face, but he rubbed his hand over his eyes more than once. I knew that move. It would not wipe away the images of whatever he had just witnessed.

Yes, your grandmother has been called. She is probably on her way.

It is a terrible thing to lose a patient.

I reassured him that I understood. I thanked him. I commiserated. I felt his pain.

I never did go inside that ICU. I ran away. But it was no longer urgent. It had never been urgent. He had been dying for most of my life.

I met my grandmother in the hospital foyer. We came in through opposite entrances: she from the street, I from the bowels of the hospital. Unlike the rest of the building, the foyer had high vaults, white columns, and a floor more suited to a museum than a hospital. Old in a way that invoked better days, not decrepitude. I moved towards her, intending to embrace her, but she
covered her face in her hands and stiffened, stepping away from me.

I didn't know what to say. Or do.

"You're no help. What's the use of being a doctor?" she said, still not looking at me, before she walked away.

The question has haunted me since.

George Looney

Wayward Guardian Angels

They like to fuck with the technical
gadgets of TV's Ghost Hunters,

whispering nonsense the men believe
to be the dead trying to tell them

something, to score big in Sweeps week.
Black and white film noirs from the forties

and fifties keep them up late, seeing
themselves lurching from shadowed alleys

to the haggard niches of doorways
where desperate lovers have whispered

sentences in one another's ears
the rest of us know only get said in films

where everything's scripted. Spontaneity
can't be said to breathe in black and white,

especially when an organ's playing
desperate hymns in the distance too flat

to be authentic, and the woman's lips seem
red even in black and white, more real

than anything she says. Saints, it turns out,
can't bluff. Angels take them to the cleaners

in poker. Their winnings get them time off
so they can hang out with the living

where they watch repeats of the old films
they know by heart. They love how

we let ourselves forget the imagination
is a kind of memory. The angels aren't

looking out for the living. They are
watching over the dead, who can't do anything

for themselves anymore. Until the day
the dead are called out of the earth

by a single note blasted on a horn
by an archangel's breath, the angels are

responsible for the dreams the dead dream.
The angels are partial to ghost stories,

and both the recent dead and the long dead
find it easy to get into tales of haunting.

Some remember late night television
from before cable, before satellite TV.

All those Vincent Price films, or Lon
Chaney, father and son. Ghost stories help

the dead feel at home in the earth.
It's the living the angels like to fuck with,

pretending to be the dead and whispering,
just barely audible, a name or a phrase,

broken and mangled a bit, just enough
to keep it from being any sort of proof.

Jonathan Greenhause

Because knowledge

is the soul of wit. Because brevity's
too brief. Because 9 stitches

can be mended. Because sliced bread
grows moldy. Because your guess

could be horrendous. Because
thoughts aren't bought

for a penny. Because
as soon as you're dead, you'll be

caught. Because neither of you
can tango. Because no cloud

stores silver. Because I'm feeling a bit
over the weather. Because the doubt

deserves no benefit. Because madness
lacks a method. Because the cat

appears to enjoy its time
in the bag. Because all your eggs

fit in a single basket. Because
these boring times

call for boring measures. Because teeth
have no skin. Because thunder

can't be stolen. Because, when you get
to the bridge, it isn't there yet.

Ramona Reeves

Sugar Land

My neighbor Mr. Andy turns on his garden hose and adjusts the nozzle. His hose unreels as he moves toward the waist-high hedge of iceberg roses that separates our yards. He wears pleated khaki pants, a plain white t-shirt and the usual navy-blue suspenders. Military men wear belts, I've often thought, like in the photo of my youthful dad before they dropped him in a jungle stung with minefields. But then I've wondered if Mr. Andy, who fought in that same war, returned home feeling cut in two, feeling he needed suspenders and breathing room when he realized he'd survived.

I know Mr. Andy only from conversations between our yards in the sweet-as-it-sounds city of Sugar Land, Texas, where they still make sugar and keep plenty of our brand on the shelves. He worked at the plant for years, often gave me a two-pound bag before the holidays, but in the eight years we've been neighbors, he's rarely invited me into his house and I've rarely invited him into mine. His wife, a petite woman with fake orange hair, is friendly enough. She comes and goes, is active in helping the poor and saving the world and such. At forty-five, I'm young by comparison and busy with life. I sell insurance. I run. I belong to clubs.

I'm watering my tomato plants when Mr. Andy draws near. Though it's early in the evening to be watering, it calms me of late. My version of lying in a hammock. "How's the new knee," I ask him.

"Well, Nate," Mr. Andy replies, "better'n the old one."

I reach down and slap one of my own knees, bony but solid below my dark gym shorts. "Running isn't good for them, but I can't see quitting."

"You'll quit when you need to," Mr. Andy replies. "When it comes right down to it, the body calls the shots."

I'm hoping exercise makes a difference. Like Mr. Andy, my

dad worked one job for forty years, but then four months ago—only days after his retirement bash—his heart gave out. No knee replacements or adventures for him. I was eating lunch when my mother called to tell me the news. She'd found him collapsed near his lawn mower with half the yard unmowed. I worry lately I'll go next, but my wife is always telling me I'm not my dad. I exercise, don't smoke, seldom drink, no pre-existing conditions. Any life insurance policy would consider me a good risk. I coach the worried voices in my head, reminding them I'm strong as can be. Somedays I do a better job of coaching them than others, but I work at controlling my feelings and letting them know who's boss.

"Fine day," Mr. Andy comments.

"Sure is." And I mean it. In this neighborhood of shade-tree lawns in a big, big state, the sun rightly shines and the blue above opens into miles and miles of possibility. The tomatoes are coming in good this year. There'll be plenty of Texas Big Boys to preserve.

Mr. Andy runs the thumb and index finger of his free hand up and down one suspender. He repeats this motion when he's watering, and I wonder if some part of him is back in the factory loading bags of sugar into crates, just as my dad loaded dairy onto ships day after day at the docks.

"Hey, I been meaning to ask," he says, "me and the wife are driving up to the Hill Country next weekend to see the grandkids. You mind watering my garden?"

He tends a big patch of tomatoes, squash and okra in the back.

"Glad to," I reply.

He thanks me, and I nod. Our conversation lags. Water gurgles from my hose, birds chirp and a distant weed whacker buzzes, but these noises can't replace the comfort of small talk. I babble about my daughter in Dallas who got married last year. I mention my son who's halfway through his time in College Station, even though Mr. Andy knows we're Aggies through and through. I tell him my son is more video gamer than gardener, that he's busy with school and can't visit very often. I get it, I say. Life takes over. I don't tell him my dad lived a half hour away and I saw him once a month at most, or that my daughter visits me even less than my son. She prefers Dallas to Sugar Land, says there's more diversity and culture, like that's a reason not to visit her pops.

"How's your mother?" Mr. Andy asks.

"You know, trying to stay busy."

He stops short of the real question of how she's doing alone. I don't say she's on tranquilizers and is scared to be by herself. Maybe it's why she stayed all those years. I don't know, but I wish people would stop asking how we're doing without my dad. It's like they expect us to dwell on his passing and bury ourselves with him, like they think he was the be-all-to-end-all, but my philosophy is this: Find the positive in every situation and dwell on that. I sell life insurance, sometimes to people who are short-timers. It's a good living and has paid for both my children's college educations. I don't dwell on the dying part. I dwell on selling peace of mind, the security of knowing a spouse, kids or grandkids will be left with a little something when it's done.

"It's been nice chatting," I say, and I suppose it's been nice enough. The tomatoes are thoroughly watered, a daily must-do in June.

"You take care now," he says.

"Sure thing." I drop my gray hose near the mature plants bending under the weight of reddish-yellow fruit and cut off the water spigot next to my porch, a good car-length from Mr. Andy. When I look up, a nest of wasps clings to an eave directly above me. I can't believe I'm just now seeing them ready as rain to pour down on anyone who passes by. Live and let live, my wife would say, but she works for the city and tends to let things slide after dealing with the public all day.

I grab an insect sprayer from my shed in the back. The sprayer is an old-fashioned tin job, a cannister with a pump that slides in and out through a long handle. My son used to call it a kettle on a stick. Recalling this, I chuckle then pump and aim the sprayer at the nest, a colony as big as my open hand. I tell the wasps to say their prayers.

The nest foams, confirming my good shot. Stunned insects drop in clumps from their catacombs. Mist coils in the air, rife with the smell of furniture polish, a scent meant to hide the chemicals. I turn and notice Mr. Andy watching me from his yard. Maybe it's the heat or the mist, but my chest constricts. I cough and drop the sprayer. Wasps are scattered everywhere in the dark-green St. Augustine. From a nearby flower bed I lift a glass tube, a rain gauge, from its prongs atop a metal garden stake. My right hand scoots the tube along the ground and traps dead wasps inside the glass. Wings, whisper-thin legs and bead-like bodies measure to the four-inch mark. Not a cloud in the sky to disturb them.

I'm on one knee, lost in my thoughts, when a hand skims my shoulder. I jolt upright, nearly spilling the tube of wasps. Mr. Andy's touch is softer than his handshake.

"Didn't mean to alarm you," he says and points at the sprayer. "Don't make 'em like that anymore."

"Belonged to my dad."

"Seemed like a good man the few times we met."

I lift the sprayer, hoping this little show-and-tell will ease the pressure building in my chest. "He used to kill everything in sight with it."

I manage a laugh, despite the image surfacing in my head. My dad is young and TV-show blond with an uneven tan and biceps like baseballs when he clutches the sprayer with one hand and primes with the other. He shoots its toxins onto shrubs and roses. The smell of tar and hot rubber spoils the air, no scents to disguise them. *That's how you get the Gooks*, dad would say when he was done. I never asked why he said this, though I knew it was left over from the war. My dad wasn't a man who welcomed questions. He was a man who went to work and liked to fish, cursed when one got away. Why would anyone say such a thing to a boy? I mumble Dad's line aloud without thinking.

"I haven't heard that in a good, long while," Mr. Andy says.

I'm worried I've upset him. "It's something my dad used to say," I try to explain. I want him to know it's not the sort of thing I would say. It's not a thing anyone should say.

"Some guys used to mouth off," he tells me.

I want to ask him why, even though I know the reason. To kill someone you've never met, you'd have to turn them into something else.

"I always figured our enemy was just as scared as us," he adds and clears his throat, maybe to change the subject. He shifts his gaze toward the tube in my hand. "What're you gonna do with them wasps?"

I lean over an azalea and settle the rain gauge, wasps and all, back into its prongs. "I don't know. I just didn't want them lying dead like that all over the yard." It's a dumb thing to admit, but it's the truth. I can tell a good fib with a little practice, but I'm not the best at impromptu lying.

"I'm here if you need anything," he says. "I mean, about your dad."

I feel an opening, a clearing between us, that I can't help but step into. "You mind if I ask you a question, about the war?"

Mr. Andy's misshapen knuckles, hard as the knots of an old tree, grip his suspenders. "Not at all."

"You sleep okay?" I ask.

"Better'n most."

His lips close over his yellowed teeth, and his gray-blue eyes train themselves on a distant thought. If he's up and down some nights, he doesn't say it. As if he's remembered me, he lets go of his suspenders, rubs his palms together and slides them into his pockets. He looks at me straight on and hoists a half smile. The hedge between us seems to disappear.

"Thanks," I reply to break the silence. "Much appreciated." My words sound lacking, but what else is there to say. If I've made him uncomfortable, saying so would only make it worse.

"Any time. Any time." He pauses and scratches his chin as though he's thinking. "About what you repeated, what your dad said, we were young and thought we were doing right, not dodging our duty, but all that's best left in the past. I wouldn't repeat it."

"Yes," I say. "You're right."

Mr. Andy ambles off, and I think about my daughter. She stayed at my parents' house several weeks one summer when she was ten or eleven, and then never stayed with them again. She said, no offense, but her granddad was crazy. He scolded at her for wasting food, yelled at the TV about foreigners taking jobs, cried out in the middle of the night. I never told her the word he used to kill people and insects alike. I never told anyone. He taught me to bait a hook, make a budget, buy a car, stuffed a twenty into my hand for dates. He was proud when I started college, understanding when I quit.

I raise one hand and shout "See you later" to Mr. Andy, who's nearly inside his house. My words attempt to stake a tent that's already blown away. My throat tightens, and if that's not bad enough, my tear ducts begin making an unscheduled run. Allergies, I tell myself, and hurry toward the shed, the place I jokingly call The Sanctuary.

When I step inside, everything I've been trying to feel positive about crumbles. Dad never watched his weight or exercised. He was a bad risk, a man undone in his youth. In my mind he forever wears a ribbed tank top and primes the sprayer like he's punching an invisible force. He sprays and sprays until a fine mist descends on his vegetable garden. I beg to try the thing, and he lets me. But the pump resists, the cannister is onerous, and my hands are more suited to toy swords. I aim the wrong way. A sloppy drizzle splatters shirts and jeans strung up on our clothesline. *Try again*, he says. He grips my shoulders with giant hands and twists me rightward. My shoulders ache beneath his grasp. I feel trapped. This memory attacks, and I can't catch my breath or control the salty fluid on my face. I imagine Mr. Andy and my dad running through palm trees, bamboo stalks and vines lit with enemy fire. Sometimes, in the middle of the night, I still hear the creaky floor and my mother's heavy steps. She fixes my dad a bite to eat and tells me to go back to bed. *Dad can't sleep*, she says. She eventually coaxes him back to bed, but other things undo him: A butcher knife striking a chopping block, a neighbor building a fence, an engine backfiring. Dad fished to escape the noises of life, and when he couldn't fish, might reprimand the happy yelps of my sister and me. I recall the hole punched into the wall, my mother's embarrassment at the hardware store when she asked how to repair a hand-size breach, the shame on Dad's face when we returned home. Although I've never punched a wall, I've cursed at my kids once or twice, and that was bad enough.

My fitness watch vibrates to let me know it's 6:30. I rub my face across my sleeve and step outside right as my wife's car appears. She's never late.

Halfway between The Sanctuary and the back door, she closes in on me wearing her typical summer work clothes of a floral top, capris and flat sandals that collar her ankles.

"I killed a big nest of wasps," I say.

She shrugs, kisses me on the cheek and asks what I want for dinner.

"How about pizza?"

"Fine with me," she says. "I'm whipped." She leans in like she wants to get a good look at me. "Have you been crying?"

"It's the heat is all. I was watering plants."

In Texas, the heat can be blamed for almost anything.

"How about some iced tea then?"

I tell her iced tea sounds nice and to go on inside, that I need to double-check I locked The Sanctuary.

"I'll phone in the order," she says and disappears into our house.

I finish collecting myself, deep breaths and all, using a method I learned at a wellness seminar. *Keep to what you know*, my dad told me at his retirement party. What he knew and kept to did him or me little good. Sometimes I wonder if I knew him at all or whether he ever knew me. You'd think so after all those years. You'd think I'd stop trying to figure it out.

Tired clouds drift into view. It'll be another few hours before the sun's pink-and-orange bulb sets the horizon on fire. I inhale and count, exhale and count, then remember the wasps. I don't want my wife to find them and wonder. I circle back, swipe the rain gauge from its prongs, and empty the remains in the trash behind our house.

Emily Carter

Duet

The tall one and the plump one
Travel conjoined in my head
Inseparable and molded into a pair
Leta and Lucille, the kin-folk version
Of better-known duos
Laverne and Shirley
Thelma and Louise
Orville and Wilbur
It's hard to distinguish one from other
Other from one

The tale goes it was Lucille
Bore that boy out of wedlock
The cord twisting around his bastard neck
Choking out whatever normal he might have stumbled upon
Named him Berry
As she was bad at spelling
Leaving him to spend his days at Grandma's house
On a quilt draped over a folding lawn chair
Drooling and diapered
He loved Elvis, Richard Petty, and Jesus
Had ceramic statues of all three kings
On a shelf near the television
An altar of something for nothing
Or nothing for something

The tall one was the driver
Moving the tan Sedan back and forth
After they both got on
Second shift at the mill
Textile lint filling the orifices, and later wrinkles
Of Leta and Lucille
Forty hours, two weeks paid, and a pension

Good odds for a corporation
As fluff lungs don't stretch much beyond
Retirement age
Berry was gone by then
The kings boxed up with the decorations of advent
Every December, they watched Petty's last Daytona
And listened to *Blue Christmas*
Still believing in the miracle of the manger
Waiting for the deliverance of an afterlife
Dirt roads paved to gold across miles of promise land

Shannon Kawalec

The Growth of Us

All of the time spent together,
Borrowed time from busy days.
Caught in the moments,
Defined by our choices,
Educated by experiences,
Fluid in our movements,
Giving and taking equally.
Hearing what we wanted,
Ignoring troubles when convenient,
Justifying our pasts and baggage,
Kindling the future we hoped for.
Laughing at ourselves and each other,
Open to new experiences.
Parenting our children, pets, and each other,
Quitting selfish habits, relinquishing our pride,
Rallying to the needs of our new family,
Shoring up our defenses,
Taming our inner demons for good,
Unflinching in our desire to do better, be better.
Valuing each other for who we are, what we've shared,
Walking hand in hand towards tomorrow.
Xyris bloom in our wake,
Youth not mourned but missed,
Zenith reached much later than expected.

Carolyn Willis

Reunion

I come from a family of no great achievement in our Blueridge mountain town, or anywhere else for that matter. The best that can be said about us is we find the grit to keep going. Every day we each rise from a warm bed, plunk tired feet down on the floor, and say, "Well, now, it could be worse." Some innate gear cranks up in our psyche, yanks our strings, and like soldier puppets, we arm ourselves for the daily grind. We don't question this trait, but we do count on it.

We're not a touchy-feely family, not churchy. We don't whine much, don't pry or impose, don't cook up intrigues, or try to change each other. We're getting older, and any indents we pressed into ourselves to accommodate one another's bulging eccentricities were shaped long ago. We each know that keeping the farms going, getting to work every day, and fixing dinner takes up all the steam any of us have left.

We're a lot like these mountains all around us. We stand side-by-side, each at our own altitude, part of the same chain and name, but when the fog drifts between us, when the clouds gather, or the dark descends, we are each alone with whatever it is that will wear us down to dust. Any compromise we negotiate with our midnight blues is a private contract.

The main thing, the most important thing, is to keep trying because some miracle is bound to turn up. We have a grim hopefulness, a steadfast expectation of better times, a kind of redneck mysticism. When everything and everybody around us is a big disappointment, we turn inward or to the land for consolation. For the most part, that's been enough to even our odds in a wily universe.

That's why we were all unprepared for Leah.

We didn't have a clue as to how deep her emptiness went, how she was scooped out hollow, so wiped clean that even the 'just-do-it' gear was stripped slick. We didn't know she had nothing to grab on to and climb hand-over-hand out of her pit—didn't know she was so far down in the dark.

The last time I'd seen her, she'd been only three, a rosy-cheeked giggler with a head full of shiny, blond curls. How the hell had she become the palest creature I'd ever seen, a thick-limbed ghost slow-motioning through the fast-paced, crowded airport? Her skin had a clammy, puffy pallor, and I remember thinking if she stood naked in the snow, no one would see her. Even her lips were bloodless, cold strips of flesh protruding from below her long nose. She was tall like us, but her hips and legs had already succumbed to her father's genetics, and big, frumpy bulges pushed against her jeans.

Her eyes were blue, her best feature, and they had an intermittent sparkle of great intelligence. But her tired, dishwater-blond hair, cut in a dismal fashion that clumped forward onto her drawn face, almost hid them.

A startled, hesitant smile rippled her pale lips when she spotted us coming toward her, as if we were a pride of hungry lions lunging down the savannah, and she, the lone straggler of a doomed herd. We'd turned out in force, our number around twenty, to lock our strong arms about her and never let her go, the baby daughter torn from us by her father thirty years before—kidnapped, taken, disappeared without a footprint.

His family had stonewalled my sister, Alice, as she beat her twenty-four-year-old fists against their seamless belief in his lies. Somewhere out there, hidden by their mute barrier, Leah had grown up believing her mother was dead.

We'd dressed up some to honor this occasion, but I could see in Leah's eyes that we were her last resort, a desperate, forced landing in a foreign country she'd rather not explore.

No matter that *we* were the missing muscle fiber in her body, the red blood eager to ruddy those pallid cheeks.

No matter that my sister has lain sleepless in her bed for thirty years, wide-eyed, tearless, staring up into the dark, wondering where her little girl is, wondering if she needs her.

No matter that Alice has hardened against the ache of it, but still dreads the night that might bring it all down on her again.

No matter any of this, Leah didn't want us like we wanted her.

I could see it, and I hoped Alice couldn't.

I glanced sideways at my sister, saw her swift breath, her wet eyes, and then I looked to the rest of the family. Between the slow blinks, the nods, the settling of expectant faces, a curtain came down, and I knew, with the instinct of the hive, that we'd all decided to ignore Leah's hapless attempt at glad reunion.

It just didn't matter, and as our long lost girl trudged lonely on toward us, we washed over her, a great wave of family.

Evan Benedict

Stealing Poems

tends to be the easiest way to write
no need to worry about inviting comparisons

lift the scarecrows'
lanky frames
from their posts
drag them snapping
through corn stalks
boneless limbs flailing
wildly and set them
on your porch
to watch the sunset
button eyes
and crooked smiles

leaning together
headpiece filled
with straw.

Kenneth Chamlee

First Crossing

Albert Bierstadt leaves New Bedford, MA,
to apprentice in Europe

I am learning sea-love, its whispers
and lulls, nudge of wind, spray-quickened face
and a stern sky ablaze. But this love
rips wave troughs deep as Berkshire ravines,
throws spears of lightning and passengers
to the rail gripping cleats and rag dreams
as water sweeps away all that is
loose, like prayers of the just-converted.

Mid-passage is a blank, sketchless gray;
trifling swells shrug by with lips of foam
as quietly as milk-whiskered cats.
Will my teacher think me apt or rude?
I left my close world, my brothers' jokes,
Mother wound with worry I would drown,
be pressed into the Dutch navy, or
worse, wed a Methodist and defect.

Nimble crew jump at pipes and whistles
to stow the jib, unhook a fouled line,
their every swing and step gauged for risk
in the rigging tied as seine for stars.

Jerome Newsome

Wooden Poles

Wooden poles splashed with rusty red separated my yard from Kendrick's. Often, we crossed those boundaries, playing hide and seek. On some days, he came outside nibbling on a piece of bologna and talking about the Baltimore Raven's game. On this particular day, his sister joined us. She towered over me. Black braids fell down her cheeks.

As I soaked in her stature, I remembered a different day, when Kendrick came outside with crimson eyes, nostrils flaring, fists balled up. I asked him what happened. He never told me then, but now he did, by standing with his head bowed against her arm. She smiled and said, "Let's play tag."

She rushed after me. I sprinted away, half-laughing, half-whimpering. She chased me through the gaps until the hard, wooden pole stood in front of me, like a defensive end. I glanced over my shoulder. Her eyebrows thundered over her eyes. She pushed me with the force of a demon possession. The pole split me. It refused my passage into Kendrick's yard.

The grass caught me. Air evacuated my lungs, shutting them down. My ears cut off, as if someone took out their batteries. My nose lost its sensitivity. My voice faded away. Every part of me grew numb. Clouds floated in the sky. They resembled boats, harboring souls destined for heaven. I remained still like a teddy bear, waiting for my boat.

His sister stared at me like a painter. She covered her mouth. Shivers surged through her. Is she not proud of what she created? Kendrick dug his fingers into his wavy, black hair, sprinkling dandruff into his teary eyes. Why didn't he get help? Why did he watch me disappear? Aren't we friends?

Something out of my vision caught their attention. They sprinted away, leaving me here. A soft, brown hand touched me. I gasped. Tears dripped out of my eyes. My mother helped me off the ground, swearing to God several times. Blood stained my shirt. She pressed a wad of paper towels onto my head and said, "Keep them there."

She rushed into the house and grabbed her keys. My sister stomped towards the wooden poles, trembling with the strength of a bear. She took off her earrings and cracked her neck. Her friend stood in her way, holding her back. Kendrick pushed his sister up the porch and slammed the door behind him.

My mother threw open the screen door and grabbed my hand. Her black apron rattled in the wind. She smelled like fries and sesame seed buns. I sat in the back of her car, jerking from how hard I cried. It seemed like I gave myself hiccups. She put her hand on the back of the passenger's seat and said, "Put on your seatbelt, honey."

I left bloody fingerprints on it, but clicked it into place. She sped down the road, telling me everything will be alright.

***

Nurses rolled me into the emergency room. The doctor jogged in front of them, talking with me and analyzing my wounds. They parked me near the wall and closed the curtain. It sealed me away from the outside commotion. He filled a syringe with a yellowish liquid.

"It's gonna feel like a bee sting, okay?"

I nodded and waited. He pressed the syringe into my eyebrow and below my nose. I grimaced. Numbness entered half of my face. Like on television, the doctor asked for various tools. A slick, thin thread moved between his fingers. It resembled dental floss. He stuck it through my bloody, open flesh, sewing it back together.

After he finished, he fetched my mother. She walked through the curtains, as if walking backstage for an exclusive interview with her new son. Is he as handsome as the previous one? Or is he unfamiliar now? Some monster made by Frankenstein? I felt uglier than I did before.

Now I have two scars to go with my wide nose and the giant mole on my chin. Now, once I walk into class, the girls will put me as number one on their list of ugly boys, rather than number five. Before I hissed into tears, my mother held me.

***

The wooden poles remained standing, like soldiers who wouldn't surrender. They manned their post, protecting both sides. We never crossed those boundaries again. I sat on the porch and stared into his yard. On most days, it's empty.

Zachariah Claypole White

During the Pandemic, I Write Letters to the Dead

Grandmother
>we breathe heavy through coffee filters
>and folded sheets
>wash our hands ivy-stung red

>i am beginning to fear the phone
>the names it must bring

Grandmother
>every night i dream a car crash
>wheels spinning in fever and thunderstorm
>our mourning spread six feet apart

Grandmother
>a child stands in the road
>watching the violence of horses
>and men
>unhurried in their grief

but Grandmother
>the rain has swept
>the worst of the pollen away

>and the redbuds bloom ferocious
>against a sky hung too low

and Grandmother
>we are still laughing

Joyce Compton Brown

Winter Wind in the Cove

How that wind swept through
with ice-gloved hands
grabbing a few trees to fling
uprooted   disturbing all those ghosts
who screamed and tried to warm
themselves by the long dead fire.
It could be the kingdom of Pompeii,
dogs and ashes and women bent for baking—
what difference a few hundred years
to that great hand of destruction
that swept Adam out of Eden
tucked Noah in an ark and drowned
his whole world so he might start
again like those farm boys did
when their daddies died again and again
in the wink of a microbe
blown down the tunnel
of somebody's frail throat?

Chloe Hillary

"Fun"eral

My navy shirt-dress is undone to my navel and I am trying to cover my nipple that Audrey is refusing, while screaming and arching her back so I can't let her go to put myself away. I have baby spew on my shoulder and the buttons at the bottom of my dress are also coming undone one by one towards my crotch. I am in the aisle seat and there are two large men sitting in my row, another across the aisle. All politely and discreetly not looking, but their mass and being radiate and fill the space around us, nonetheless.

My alarm was set for 5.30 am this morning to make the 8.00 am flight – factoring a feed before we left and time for me to cobble together a respectable outfit from my very limited number of clothes that fit me, and to put on make-up for the first time in three months. No mascara. But of course, Audrey woke at 4.30 am, and so that is when this day started. Now on that flight, with only one coffee in my system and a small piece of fruit toast, Audrey does eventually give in to the hum of the plane and drift off and I can steel myself for the day ahead.

I remember when I arrived at the Brisbane airport for the first time, seven years ago and Kat was there to greet m, in her old silver Toyota Corolla, all the windows manually wound down. We drove from the airport to her house without a moment of silence, she mostly filled it with bubbly chatter about the city, about work, about life. I remember feeling a great sense of gratitude to have Kat back in my life and to be back in hers. I remember an optimism for all the adventures we would have together in a new city.

There is a distinctive thickness to the air every time you step off a plane in Brisbane, and today the thickness clings to my heart and weighs my limbs down. I haven't been back since Kat and David's wedding. That was three years ago. Kat had lost her hair after her first round of chemo. It had grown back through the fluffy phase and she wore it in a pixie cut.

The transition from the plane to the rental car and to the venue goes smoothly. A brief interjection for a poo in a just changed nappy, but nothing too derailing. I type the location into google and it tells me it's a wedding venue and that it's probably closed today.

I find my crew when I arrive. Five women none of whom I have seen for three years or more, since the wedding. We all have children now, theirs all older and at home. After covering off the general "how are you holding up?" and "how's work? Where are you now?", the children is where the conversation goes. I can't remember what we would have spoken about five years ago, Kat would have taken care of that, but now it is a natural, easy topic. *Billy's started school, Charlotte's still sleeping terribly, River asked me when I'm going to die.*

I find a spot in the aisle near the door. Before the service starts, I am absent mindedly patting Audrey's nappied bum and looking around the room, trying to remember the names of people I haven't thought of in years. On the screen at the front there is a beautiful photo of a maybe 10-year-old Kat, balancing on the roots of a huge fig tree, in a haphazard colourful outfit that an adult Kat would have worn. Bright sneakers, with a clashing A-line skirt and a t-shirt with an unidentifiable print, tucked into the waistband. Her name and lifespan printed below; *Katherine Renee Peters 07.12.84 to 13.03.21.*

Under the screen is a huge wicker basket, the lid sagging slightly under the weight of an impressive bouquet of native flowers. It occurs to me for the first time that Kat is in there. I know she's dead, I know this is her funeral, but it had not for one second occurred to me that her body would be here. For some reason this seems like a given at an old person's funeral but unspeakable when they were so young.

I saw her only two days before she died, and her body hardly looked like her own then. Bloated and unmoving, completely reliant on other people for sustenance and protection. I got a horrible pulling feeling in my chest to think about what it must look like in there now, two weeks later. I try not to think about it as I rearrange Audrey's chubby limbs so they're not dangling into the aisle as people walk past to find their seats. I focus on the basket and think about how the flowers complement the wicker, and then I wonder if she had chosen them.

Kat's best friend from primary school gives the eulogy. She is calm and composed. Heroic. She tells stories that encapsulate Kat's approach to life. She says that she had lived large but dreamed bigger, which makes her sound like an underachiever, but nothing could be further from the truth, she says. She just had some wild dreams.

As I listen to stories about her life, some I know, some take me by surprise, I wonder if she was born to die young. She lived such a big, full life. Maybe she was just fitting it all in before she had to go. I lower my nose onto Audrey's head, her fluffy hair like felt brushing my skin, tears streaking my foundation, and reflect on what lies before her. I hope for her that she has someone in her life like Kat.

One story about Kat's life that only I know, is the time Kat told me she wanted kids. It was before I was pregnant, but we were talking about the future, in the attentive way Kat had. I could go to her with any problem or question, and we would talk it out, look at it from every angle, until we had whittled it down to a plan. We were talking about the parenting style of the woman who is speaking now. Kat had an opinion. She had an opinion about everything. She was too generous to say it, but I knew. Then she told me that she was looking forward to seeing how my husband and I managed the "parenting thing", she thought we would approach it in a sensible way, like she would. I have thought of that so many times since becoming a mother.

The friend finished with an amusing story about a skit involving clowns who mistakenly end up at a funeral, thinking it was a "fun"eral. Everyone claps, in confirmation that this is a celebration of life. And Audrey wakes. I grip her body as she squirms. Pull her into my chest and look into her eyes as they flick open, vacant and dark, checking for me and flutter shut like an unused tissue drifting to the floor.

I can only see the back of Kat's mum's head, through the crowd, standing next to David at the front of the grand room. I'm selfishly pleased that I can't see her face. I don't know how I could stand before a mother saying goodbye to her daughter while I hold my new daughter in my arms. I know now in my newly forming mum-bones, how unfathomable it is to let a daughter go; how every cell in her body would be wishing that she was holding her daughter now. I slide my index finger into Audrey's fist, hanging loosely by her side and she grips on to it.

After the service the basket is wheeled down the aisle towards the front of the grand old house. There is an awkward moment where everyone sits, not knowing what to do, before someone thinks to mention that we should follow the coffin. We all dutifully fall into a line and follow the basket out the front. The hearse awaits on the gravel road with its rear and one side gaping open, the wicker basket already inside. The road is rimmed with a waist high, perfectly manicured hedge, holding back a dozen graceful gum trees.

With Audrey in one arm I grab a small handful of petals from the basket next to the hearse with my spare arm and press them onto the lid of the coffin and silently whisper, goodbye. She should be out here. This is her party.

I stand amongst the mourners on the gravel on the other side of the hearse, facing the house. Everyone is silent, heads bowed. And then Audrey starts wailing. Like she's letting out the grief everyone else is self-consciously holding in. Screaming and squirming and thrashing. I pat and jig and shush and chatter and nothing is placating her. She wants milk. I'm using both of my arms to wrestle her, I have a bag on my back and I'm standing in the middle of a group of people in a big open space, on gravel. There is nowhere to feed her. On the porch of the house there are some benches, but the hearse is between me and the house and between the hearse and the house Kat's mother and brother are huddled together, blocking the stairs. My only options are to stand in the middle of everyone and let her scream, or push my way through the crowd, past the hearse and past the mourning family and sit in full view of everyone and get my boob out. So she screams, and I sweat from embarrassment and the physicality of trying to keep her in my arms. I want to scream too.

When the hearse is gone, I walk a little quicker than the general shuffle of the crowd back up the steps to one of the benches and try to give her milk, which she mostly refuses again, as everyone files past me and inside. Most people glance my way with varying degrees of pity and judgment.

After the service, once Audrey has composed herself, we sway around the room, Audrey drifting off to sleep while I say polite hellos. There are a lot of people here I know or at least had known for a season of my life. Good people. Kat's people.

"Are you thinking about number two yet?" Amanda, ex-colleague, mother of two, asks in a playful but I sense serious way.

"We'll see how we go with this one first." I let out an awkward chuckle.

"I don't want to scare you but my oldest is 7 and I'm only just starting to feel like I'm coming out of the bubble. You know, the parenting bubble. Being here and thinking about Kat makes me wonder if I've made the right choices."

Amanda's not finished, but before she can explain, a woman I have never seen before is gently pulling on my elbow to tell me that I did a good job during the ceremony, staring at Audrey instead of me. Perhaps she's talking to Audrey not me. Since Audrey can't respond I thank her, not certain about the content of her compliment, but keen to move the conversation on, I ask her how she knew Kat. Her answer is dull and leads nowhere and we stand staring at each other until she offers to get me something to drink and when I politely decline, she shuffles off.

By then Amanda has moved on to another conversation so I return to my original circle of mums. I wanted to talk to Amanda about my choices. I had been plagued by feeling that I had drifted away from Kat since getting pregnant, for fear of upsetting her. I hid my bulging belly and then my new human from her, I didn't want to boast that my life was moving forward while hers was stalling; that I could have the family that she always wanted, but she couldn't even have her life. Maybe that wasn't even what Amanda was getting at. The conversations return to the generic and mundane.

Leaving felt strange. I probably wouldn't see many of these people again, my only connection to them being Kat. There was nothing to say but goodbye. No future. No plans. But I guess that was the essence of a funeral.

I check in for my flight home at 4.28 pm, check in closes at 4.30 pm. The women are adoring, too old to be parents of babies, too young to be grandparents, and move us to the front of the plane and block out a seat next to us.

I speed through the terminal with Audrey strapped to my front, thankfully quiet and compliant. Security. Nappy change. No time for toilet. Kit-Kat. Gate. Plane.

The woman across the aisle has long unkempt fingernails and is wearing leggings with thick black fluffy socks pulled over the ankles, jammed into open sandals. She's wearing an oversized thick cable knit with a high neck and a half zip up the front, cream with a deep navy v-shape around the collar. Her hair is greasy and in a messy bun and she has obviously fake eyelashes with the remains of yesterday's make up still on her face. She spends the whole flight zooming in and out of a photo on her phone, of her and another woman, in slinky formal wear with obnoxious fake tans and high heels. Zooming in, touching up her lips, zooming out. Zooming in, touching up her hair, zooming out. Zooming in, touching up her arms, zooming out. Her hair, in the photo long, ash blonde and straight, receives most of the attention and the friend on her arm receives very little.

Did I do that to Kat? Did I leave her on my arm, imperfect and unwell, while I perfected my own life? A new city, a baby. Moving forward, improving. I couldn't have changed anything for her. I can't measure how much she changed me.

Audrey will not eat. She screams for take-off, I pat, and jig and shush while she stares back at me with huge eyes until all of a sudden, they roll back in her head and she is asleep. Her little body surrendered. Defeated, exhausted. I pull out my earphones, trying to move only my spare arm and not my body so as not to wake her, and put my audiobook on and try hard to focus on that and not on the zooming going on to my left. Not on my life choices. Not for now.

Joan Barasovska

Carrying Clare

Mystery conceived in passion
spreads a tent inside my body,
scoops out space
I'd blithely claimed as mine.

I grow heavy with her campsite
and the gear we've taken on.
After work each day I buy
a secret chocolate éclair
and eat it at Nelson's Bakery,
where I'll soon show off my baby.

Her father grants me
naming rights if it's a girl.
On a cold day at the beach,
jacket straining to span my belly,
with one booted foot I trace
her name in giant letters
in wet sand: CLARE.

I pray this hidden daughter,
now assembling all she'll require,
will live to be my better self,
take chances I could never take.
I pray for a safe birth.
I pray to be the mother she will need.

Her father and I wait for March.
He says she could easily be a boy.
Our daughter's eyes, not yet open,
greedily seek mine.

Sam Barbee

Hands to Myself

hands make us human . . .
Aristotle

Our kitchen, where your aprons droop. I stir,
stir the strings; snag, snag the loops. They help
me still witness, witness you. Blue fantasia, true faith
in aloneness, in violet depth. Flocks blot, blot
sun's final lap, help prepare, prepare night's profile:
a nudge, nudge into our past.

I smooth, smooth the mattress but cannot make it moan,
moan. I grasp, grasp the closet door to curate clothes
dreaming, dreaming of usefulness. Clutter of robes, fashions
arranged, arranged per seasons. The inappropriate shoved,
shoved back, idle in the tidy dark. Old permissions
cross, cross my anxious palm.

I clench, clench basic routines at your grave – pretend
to sift, sift fingers through your hair. Iron, iron your lace
across the headstone. Press, press so delicately. Hands
not yet learned, learned how to keep, keep you real.
A startling departure of some stupid birds –
their flying, flying, always in human terms.

Crysta Parkinson

The Anchor Inn Motel

In the days when Madonna's raunchy "Justify My Love" music video being whispered about among blushing sixth graders was the most erotic reference in my life, the seeds of an unlikely friendship were planted.

*　*　*

The motel where Kay and her infant daughter, Sterling, lived was three doors down from the two-story white house where my best friend Austine's family lived, and one August night Austine and I had spread an old patchwork quilt on the lawn to watch a meteor shower. Austine and I were tossing peanut M&M's into each other's mouths from opposite sides of the blanket when a woman in a black leather mini skirt walked by, red hair teased into defiance of gravity, pushing a baby in a stroller. She said hello, I fawned over the baby, and before the meteors started flying, I had an offer of a new babysitting job. Soon I was curled up with Sterling in their motel room a couple of nights a week, and finding a confidante in her easy-going (if slightly scandalous) mom.

*　*　*

Summer rolled into fall, and adventures in the neighborhood faded to days at a desk. The moment I was released from my seaside middle school for the day, I would race home to check in, then walk to the motel.

It is six blocks from school to home and another 10 blocks from the two-bedroom house our family of five lived in on Mitchell Avenue to the low-slung beige motel. The sign has boasted "new management" since the eighties, just one of many ways in which the cinder block building is frozen in time. Like every motel in Blaine, Washington, the Anchor Inn Motel has a million dollar view of Drayton Harbor, but unlike the others, no brochures claim the marvel.

This was the sort of place people go to overdose or bounce

back from divorce. This was not a place to enjoy a holiday on the coast. If a tourist accidentally found themselves with a booking, I imagine they would have made it about as far as the buckling parking lot before realizing the error of their ways and pointing the station wagon back onto Peace Portal Drive in search of more appropriate accommodation — or maybe a place to park and sleep in the backseat.

* * *

Getting to Kay's was on my mind that afternoon as I cut across my front lawn. I picked my way through the rotting landmines dropped in the sparse grass by the wild branches of the faithful old pear tree widely flung above, then paused on the narrow porch to listen for clues to what might be happening inside. I liked to know what I was getting myself into, but no luck. Silence met my ears.

The weathered skeleton of the flimsy aluminum screen door bent awkwardly as I held it with my hip and turned the knob on the front door a millimeter at a time to avoid noise as I slipped inside. As my eyes adjusted from the bright afternoon to the tiny darkened living room, I saw Mom was lying on the autumn-hued velour of the hand-me-down couch, brown hair splayed over a pillow, Strawberry Shortcake blanket pulled to her chin, damp washcloth covering her forehead and eyes.

The heavy brown drapes were drawn tightly against the day, a skirt hanger clamping them together with all it had to offer. The slimmest sliver of light still made its way through, illuminating a single line across the hifi stereo console opposite the couch and adding a horror movie quality to the shadowy room.

I deposited my backpack on the lone chair and went to the bathroom for a fresh washcloth. I let the water run until it was cold, then soaking the cloth and ringing it out with a practiced, careful hand. Five steps back to the couch, my eyes adjusting now to the darkness. She didn't move when I replaced her warmed cloth with the new one. I tiptoed toward the door.

"Where are you going?" she asked, her voice gravel.

"Kay and Sterling's."

Mom lifted the cloth enough to get one accusatory cerulean eye on me. "You're going to babysit for the hooker again?"

I cringed, but bit back a sarcastic reply. I knew better than to push back if I wanted to be at the Anchor Inn by four. Instead I stood still, the doorknob rough in my hand, waiting to see what her mood would dictate. Would it be a list of chores before I could leave the house? A rant about where I spent my time? The unknown held me in suspense.

"Put your backpack away," she said, and dropped the cloth back over her eye.

I moved as quickly as I could to pick my backpack up and sling it over my shoulder on the way out the door before the request could grow.

* * *

As I circumvented the knee-high fence posts and stepped onto the uneven sidewalk that doubled as motel patio, a flurry of activity from an open door drew my attention inside, where three men sat and stood in a room which somehow simultaneously mirrored Kay's and looked nothing like it. A short man with a gap-toothed grimace and stained wife beater moved to the doorway to gesticulate and leer. I rolled my eyes as I stepped around him.

I knocked on the bronze door of room eight and it was opened almost immediately by a woman in her mid-30s wearing a black lace bra and leather mini skirt. Kay turned on one bare heel and went back to teasing her red hair to just the right level of wild in front of the mirror, which hung over a dresser covered in makeup and hair products. Incense burned into a precarious line of ash over a wooden tray on an end table, the scent mingling with the smell of hairspray and musty curtains in my nose.

"How was school?" she asked over the Bon Jovi ballad that filled the room.

The carpet was loud, thinning, the color of a peacock. It clashed comically with the garish metallic green and gold of the polyester bedspread 12-year-old me didn't yet know to avoid at all costs. The bed was piled with board books and stacking toys that bounced into the air as I plopped myself in their midst.

"It was alright."

She turned and looked at me, her eyes narrowed, searching, as though examining just beneath my skin. "Just alright?"

I shrugged.

She asked about my World History test as the song "You Give Love a Bad Name" faded to "Livin' On a Prayer."

"It went fine. Better than expected," I said.

I leaned over the edge of the bed to peer between the peeling white bars of the half-sized crib where Sterling was asleep, her chubby little cheek pressed against the stars on the flannel sheet and her bottom in the air.

"It always does. I don't know why you let yourself get so anxious about these things," she said, and turned back to the magic she was casting with her round brush and hair spray.

That was a deeper conversation than I was ready to have. I watched the rise and fall of the baby's breathing.

"Did you bring that poem for me to read?" Kay asked.

I rummaged through my backpack and pulled out a composition book, flipped it to a page marked by a yellow post-it.

Kay glanced at the clock and swapped me the notebook for a bottle of fire engine red nail polish. "Paint me while I read? I'm going to be late," she said, and settled down on the bed beside me.

I appreciated her not pointing out I needed a distraction to keep from having an anxiety attack while she pored over the words. I kept my eyes focused on the hand she placed on my backpack between us and shook the bottle of polish.

Several times as she read, she snapped the fingers of her free hand. "Yes, girl!" she announced as she finished. "Yes!"

Focusing on her perfectly almond-shaped nails, I brushed

on first one coat of the red lacquer and then a second as Kay thoughtfully workshopped my poem. She offered ideas for a stanza that wasn't quite working, brainstormed words to replace a weak phrase. When I was done, she blew on her hands until she was satisfied the paint was set and then donned a sheer blouse.

"How do I look?" she asked, spinning in the center of the room, bangles chiming on outstretched arms.

I offered my approval, feeling like it mattered what I thought.

She sprayed the air with Giorgia Beverly Hills and walked through it. "Come, come," she said, and spritzed a second time for me to step through.

I mimicked her steps and was rewarded with a bouquet of bergamot and apricot on my skin and in my hair.

"I'll be back in time for curfew," she said, meaning mine. She stepped into her stiletto heels, slipped a folded twenty into her bra and blew me a kiss, as she slipped out the door.

I pulled a book from my bag and propped the pillows behind me, settling in to read *Pride and Prejudice* until Sterling woke up from her nap.

* * *

It was drizzling as I slipped from the motel room later that night. Kay had offered to give me a ride home, but Sterling had played hard and fallen back to sleep, so I didn't want her to have to take her out. Besides, we both knew my mom and step dad wouldn't like it.

I had no idea if Kay was a sex worker, but I knew two things for sure — I didn't care, and I didn't think it was any of my parents' (or my) business. I also thought that if they really believed that she was, they probably would not have let me hang out in her seedy motel room. Yet they were sure to repeat it on every reference, and seeing her dropping me off outside would only have served to feed their judgment. So I walked.

From the porch I could hear my parents laughing at *Carol*

Burnett, and I knew that meant I wasn't late. My mother told time by what was on television. *Roseanne* was Tuesdays at 9 p.m. *The Cosby Show* was Thursdays at 8. Gerald McRaney's *Major Dad* was the closest thing to discussion of the Gulf War as we ate in front of the TV, plates balanced on folding knees. And on Friday nights, the end of *The Carol Burnett Show* signaled my 10 p.m. curfew.

Mom was still wrapped in the Strawberry Shortcake blanket, but she was sitting up on the couch now, her feet curled beneath her and my step dad sitting at the other end, beer in hand. He looked up and reminded me to lock the door behind me. Her eyes stayed on the screen as I went down the hall and shut myself in my bedroom to listen to *Rhoda at Night* on Z95.3.

* * *

A year later, Kay had secured a run down duplex with tin siding nestled in the elbow of Interstate 5. It was tiny but quiet, the last house on a dead-end street surrounded by newer, larger homes. She made an effort to put down roots in that shabby home at 950 Cedar Street the moment she set foot inside. Even if they were the shallow surface roots of a willow, for the sake of her little girl she was intentional about feeding those roots like they already represented a mighty oak. Their stint of homelessness faded in the rearview, and she built them a new life.

Kay filled every corner of the cozy space with herself, chasing the cold of damp Washington days away with funky thrift store finds. Colorful tapestries lined the walls — trees of life, vibrant mandalas, elephants and galaxies. Thick candles dripping with wax and sticks of musky incense lined well-considered eclectic furniture, clothes spilled from an overfilled closet. (Where had those been when she lived in the motel?) The new home was on my way home from school, so I would stop by more afternoons than not to play with 18-month-old Sterling and conference with her mother.

At home, I emulated her style in my own, once spartan, bedroom. In contrast to the neglected rooms and empty taupe walls of the rest of the house, my room was filled with bright knick-knacks and vaguely Buddhist tapestries — purchased with crumpled dollar bills and never failing to draw my mother's side-eye. I burned incense until my step-dad burst through the door to see if I was smoking weed, then switched to vanilla-scented candles. I listened to the radio and read books Kay had mentioned. I worked at having something smart to discuss, to form considered opinions she would approve of.

Of course, it wasn't just my inner decorator that Kay fed. She fed my budding feminist, my nascient novelist, my intentional self-analyzer. She encouraged me to think through the ideas forming in my adolescent brain — to articulate them, to put them on paper. We listened to the hair bands she adored, she played interlocutor as we discussed what I was reading and writing, and I felt safer there than in the house of surprises that met me on the other end of Mitchell Avenue. She didn't own a TV and didn't seem to miss it, but she did have an antiquated three shelf bookcase that held her greatest treasures.

* * *

Kay's attentiveness set off a mentor-seeking pattern that would continue throughout my life, as I found myself looking for figures to fill gaps left by a complicated relationship with my mother and step dad, the absence of my father. Some of the most valuable interactions I have had in the decades since could be directly attributed to her planting an open-mindness about what meets the eye versus what people have to offer.

Another year and we would have both moved on — her and toddler Sterling to a town further down the coast, me to eighth grade and the mentorship of an English teacher who helped me to publish my poetry in *Stone Soup*.

Was she perfect? Hell no. But maybe one of the best lessons from my relationship with Kay is that we're all complex characters, we're all deep and messy and a collage of things pieced together. She was juggling more than enough baggage of her own, but stopped to help me to carry mine for a while, offering the unconditional support I craved, the interest in who I was and what I was up to.

And that was more than enough to make my love completely justified.

George Looney

Rituals in Lingerie and Insomnia

Dressed in the lingerie of the emphatic, the moon
entices this storm to let everything go. South
of here, a woman slips into a black camisole and grins

at the idea of any man trying to ignore his nature
getting drunk in a tavern where the dust of the exotic
is nightly wiped off the bar. It's been said nothing is

more elegant than the curve, in the right light,
of a woman's hip bones. In the black camisole,
the woman could well be mocking the moon

and its desperate and feeble attempts at luridness,
or she could be paying homage. So often
nothing more than intent separates what we love

and what we tolerate. The saying is, the woman
has a compromising photo of the moon.
If you're willing to pay what she asks, you can

see it. When she slips the blurred photo out of
the waist of her jeans, past the hieroglyph for
passion the curve of her hip bone's become, you

don't have a chance. You'd pay anything for
just a glimpse. It's the moon, after all,
and many have been maddened by the longing

for her luminescent body. She has often been
blamed for everyone being out of sorts
the nights that, full of wine, she staggers through

what's left of the sky. Not even the longing
to hold the moon and keep her safe in your arms
till she sobers up excuses the gentrification of

the night sky. There's often almost nothing
between devastation and the quiet, inner lives
of men and women who only want what they've been told

to want. Longing is, in the end, every bit
as fickle as you suspected. The pornographic
moon pics were photo-shopped, and nothing you have

believed in remains free of suspicion. Off
in another country, a frail *matador de toros* shrouds
the bones, reconstructed with precision, of a bull

with his *capote*. Dust taunts the indifferent ghosts
in the stands. The moon, in a fluid Spanish,
croons a love ballad drenched in *duende*

and reminiscent of a lurid fable the woman
in the black camisole whispered in your ear
one night after sex, so explicit and so the opposite

of intimate that you cringed. You didn't want to
see the pictures she said she had, and you couldn't
imagine touching such an exquisite woman,

though her elegant clavicle and neck and chest
had gone red as a result of you having touched her.
Such rendezvous can be a side-effect of not enough

sleep, it's been said. Mundane hallucinations become
so real the waking world—where the moon is
naked and without language in the distance that is

the night sky—isn't discernible from the world
in which your three-in-the-morning house is haunted
by an ex-lover, a dead brother, and a cat whose ashes

rest in a clay vessel on the mantle. When ghosts
and visions get together, desire staggers, drunk
and muttering to itself, into the kitchen for coffee

steaming and black enough a woman could wear it
for lingerie and not be anything but irresistible—
maddening, actually. Longing haunts us more

than the dead do, more than a storm that wants to
turn us from the moon and all the lavish promises
it makes in Spanish or some long-dead language.

Mark Caskie

Showering in the Dark

The wafting steam clouds
the glass panes,
muting the alley light.
I stand naked,
groping for the soap
in its dish. Darkly,
the day washes off,
I move in a dream
of my own body, glad
to only half-see the hints
of age: the gray chest hairs,
the slackened muscles—
for once, I am Hercules.
My muscles flex to touch
where we only touch
to clean: armpits, back,
even between toes,
like an Egyptian woman,
wrapping the pharoah's feet
in balms of myrrh, or
the care of a Roman wife
whose husband has
returned from a long march,
and who prepares
to leave again tomorrow.

Edward Hagelstein

Huck Phreed

Daily set me up with a quick recording session at a studio in Miami with a country band, or what passes for a country band these days. They were called Coochdoodle, or Pinchaloaf, something like that. Baby Wampus would have been a better name. I suspected it was something he cooked up with Tallulah to keep me busy for a couple of days but it turned out to be real. The band was almost finished recording their third album but needed a pedal steel player for one song.

I'd never heard of them but did a little research. They'd had a couple of near-hits with what one kindly reviewer called "simple songs about simple pleasures." Trucks and dogs and cousins in tank-tops I assumed.

They flew me down and put me in a hotel on the beach. No complaints there. On approach, with the ochre roofs and tropical green foliage of Miami Beach and the bright aqua Atlantic below I thought how Betty didn't like to travel because she felt dowdy, poor, and out-of-place most of the time. Miami wouldn't have boosted her self-image at all. Sleekness, beauty and money were prominent. All superficial and meaningless in my opinion – or so I would have told her. I kind of liked it.

A car took me to the studio the next day. I was introduced all around and then the band ignored me. They had a pedal steel player and I wondered why I was there until I went to shake his hand and it was bandaged up. The driver told me later the guy had been bitten by a K-9 when the police went to the band's rental house to investigate neighbor's complaints that local high school girls were coming and going late at night, some in their cheerleader uniforms. Apparently the dog hit on the pedal steel player's pants when he was at the front door vociferously asserting his rights by telling the cops they couldn't come in, and when he turned to go back inside the dog grabbed his hand, which was in his pocket clutching a baggie of MDMA tabs. So he was out on bond and unable to play, but the ruckus gave the junior varsity cheerleaders time to escape out the back gate.

The driver also offered that the band had recorded their first two albums in Nashville but wanted to try Miami this time because they were going for a country-beach sound, toes in the sand, which was selling big right then, riding that questionable wave. And they heard the drugs were plentiful.

He also told me they were producing this album themselves without adult supervision, apparently one more step in an ongoing effort to involuntarily hasten their own career demise, resulting in a chaotic recording process. And all the studio people severely hated them. I told myself it was one day of well-paid work and two nights in a nice hotel.

I set up my Fessenden in the studio while the band jabbered about which hotel beach bar they were going to terrorize that night. The demo track for the song we were going to do was coming over the speakers and I recognized the work of a friend who made his living these days by writing songs for creatively deficient recording artists in his home studio outside Nashville. Apparently he just worked up the instrumental for this tune, a simple- guitar, bass, and drums arrangement, and the band was going to append their own lyrics, at their insistence.

Most musicians are not a clean-cut bunch of people in any case, myself included, but this group appeared to have dressed out of a hurricane victim donation box that morning and then crawled through a restaurant grease trap on their way to the studio. I know my hotel provided shampoo, but these guys seemed to have never heard of the stuff.

So with much hullabaloo, furtive trips outside to toke up, and discussion of their "process," they were getting ready to write lyrics. I thought it was unwise to wait until they were about to record, plus a waste of studio time. But it wasn't my band, or my money.

They stopped ignoring me long enough for the tubby bass player to turn his red-rimmed eyes my way and say I should go into the kitchen and get him a cup of coffee. Black, heavy on the sugar.

"I want my breath sweet for the jailbait later." He leered at me as if I were part of his evening plans.

Being at least a decade his senior I looked at him blankly for a few beats. A couple of the others glanced at him like they were wary of his stupidity. My first thought was to grab one of his swollen fingers and bend it back toward his wrist until I heard a snap. Since I'm a get-along guy I told him I'd be happy to do that. On my way to find the kitchen I heard him mutter something to the others about for the amount they were paying the old dude for a day's work he should make himself useful.

There were three girls at a table in the kitchen. The jailbait in question, I supposed. We said hi and they went back to what they were doing, writing on 3 by 5 cards, which I assumed to be homework while they waited for the band to finish. Hopefully college level at least. I found the coffee and poured a cup half-full. Ignoring the sugar packets on the counter, I rummaged in the cabinets until I found a large container of salt, topped it up with that, and stirred well.

I smiled when I handed him the cup and he took it without thanking me. I turned away to hear him gag and spew and turned back to see two of his bandmates wiping their faces and the spit-mist of his salt-coffee still floating down to the floor.

"What the fuck dude!" he yelled at me. "This tastes like the beach!"

I shrugged. "Must have gotten my white granules mixed up. I'm sure it's happened to you."

I went into the control room where the two sound guys, young enough that the ink on their recording arts diplomas was damp but still more professional than this band would ever be, silently gave me low fives under the view of the window as we watched the addled band looking for paper towels to wipe up the mess.

"There are still people who don't realize this world runs on a certain amount of mutual respect," I said.

The sound kids looked busy while they suppressed laughter.

Nobody asked me to run any more errands and the bass player spent the rest of the session glancing over at me like a street mutt expecting to be beaten for something, or nothing. His playing suffered for it, in my opinion. Or maybe he just wasn't any good.

Their lyric "process" turned out to be one I'd never encountered before, or since. The girls from the kitchen came in with their cards and they joined the band, sitting in a circle on the floor. I got the Fessenden in tune. I already had an idea of what I was going to do by listening to the demo track, as long as the band didn't change the key or tempo. And I didn't picture this group striving for perfection or originality so I assumed they'd take the path of least resistance by sticking to the original.

They arranged their cards with words and phrases in the center of the circle. It reminded me of third grade, except the drummer had his hand so far down the back of the pants of the girl next to him that I hoped she wiped good that day. Then they started shuffling cards around to arrange a rhyme. Curiosity got the best of me and I walked over there, whether they liked it or not. Nobody was going to challenge me at that point.

Here's some of what the girls had written. And I don't know if they got writing credit for the finished song, but I doubt it.

Thong. Bong.

Boom Boom. My Room.

Pardy. Hardy.

Tractor. Erecter. I don't know if the spelling on some of these was intentional or not.

Chicken Fries. Tight Thighs.

To the band's credit they took the cards for *Sweet* and *Meat* and tossed them aside. Probably hit a little close to home. They kept *Sexy* and *Mexi*, which caused me to involuntarily raise an eyebrow.

Rump. Pump.

Cuervo. Pervo. I kind of liked that combo.

Tight Jeans and *Lesbians*. This was probably not going to be radio-friendly.

Bail and *Jail* they threw aside. Also a sensitive subject.

Cold Beer. Dead Deer. They discussed changing that to *Cold Brew* and *My Crew*. More bro-ey. *Mamacita* and *Margarita* I thought would go for sure as being too obvious, but they put them in a place of honor near the top. There was no underestimating these guys.

After they had the semblance of a basic, dumb-sounding song, minus linking words, it was announced the taco truck was outside. When the studio was empty for almost an hour while the band and girl scribes ate and dicked around outside I got the sound guys to check my levels and record the part I'd worked out from the demo. I knew if I waited for the band it would be hours before they were ready.

The sound guys miked my amp, I set my tone and warmed up. They put the demo on a loop while I worked out my part a couple of times, then had them record.

I did three takes, each a bit different, listened as they played them back in the booth, broke the Fessenden down and told the guys to run them by the band when they got back and noticed I was gone and that I'd be in the hotel until tomorrow if they wanted something different. I wanted to be no part of their scene and knew they'd be more comfortable without me around. I flew out the next afternoon without hearing from them again. And I got paid.

The whole trip mostly took my mind off Betty for a few days.

I heard that song oozing out of a bar jukebox a year later and it sounded about as lifeless and simpleminded as you would think coming from a bunch of misspelled flashcards on a floor. It was all those guys were capable of. Except for my part. Objectively, that was good. Although buried a little low in the mix for my liking. The pedal steel elevated the tune, but not enough.

They used my second take I believe exactly as I'd played it though. I had just let it go kind of dreamy and yearning for that take. I remember my mind disengaging and drifting out of the room.

I pictured myself floating up and out over Biscayne Bay while I played. I gave that song more than it deserved, but sometimes that's the job.

I hoped they'd forgotten to list me on the credits.

Bob Wickless

The Willard E. Martin Marching Band

After the brassy engines and pumps
With their catcall and siren's scream,
After the drum major's peacock strut,
Flashing baton gauging each step,
And the slim, perfect thighs
Of the high school's majorettes,
White uniforms, gold pressed
Tight over their stiff, perfect breasts,
And the swift, tuned, precision bands
Followed by the town's luminaries—
Aldermen, Mayor, Chief of Police,
After the home spun beauty queens,
Milky girls in sleek automobiles—
Cadillacs, Lincolns, bright T-Birds,
And the local club's quivering machines—

But before the throng of children,
Gorillas, masks of rubber death,
Before the clowns with huge, flapping feet
And the tiny, gray-bearded Uncle Sams,
Before the herd of silly animals—
Horses, hind quarters oddly deranged,
Moving crossways and every which way at once,
Before giraffes, skeletons, orangutans,
And the perennial, white-sheeted ghosts
Shapeless as oozing amoebas,
Before the hobos, winos, drunks
In black face and out-of-date clothes
And the town's truer misfits—shell-shocked
Tony, Junkyard Jim, The Walnut Lady,
Bicycle Ed, The Woman with No Nose—

Comes The Willard E. Martin Marching Band.
Local trumpets, saxophones, drums
Who got no nods from College Park
To strut their stuff at half-time's game
Or rock the stage at Top Hat Bar,
But daily swing to the butcher shop
Or hardware store, the used car lot,
Beat time for time with rivet guns
And hammer the tune on worn-out cars,
Who once a year strut the stars,
The faded blues, the stripes, the bars
Of their ridiculous uniforms
To march before the smart set crowd
Who hoot and jeer and wisecrack call
The Wilted E. Martin Mocking Band.

And yet they dream as they play:
Wide avenues open up
To the snow of ticker tape
As Hank wails like Louie, Dan,
Enthralled, raps Gene on pearl drums,
And Willie works arthritic joints
Into miraculous Benny G. glides
That make the fire engines disappear,
And the dignitaries, their shiny cars,
Even the farm queen, with a sudden *poof*
Of her powder, gone, and the high
School gods and goddesses, all gone,
Everyone gone but the ragamuffins
And the children, who strut and stride,
Glide with the Martin Marching Band.

Then how they wail! How youth and age
Conspire! How the hacking of beef
Does not matter, how cars
Can sell or not sell themselves,

And the world is not just hard-
Ware, but filled with mystery
And purpose and pride—how all eyes
Are upon them—admiration flows
Like rain in slick gutters
And the shiny horns glitter, cry
Until it is no use. Reality crashes
Like a lamp struck by packed ice.
Other bands are performing feats
Martin can't imagine. Sirens scream,
The right world quickens, electrifies—

Until no harmonies are appropriate,
No music or words will suffice
This sadness, the simple truth
Of old age, naked and graceless
And dreamless, beyond all disguise.

Kenneth Chamlee

At the Metropolitan Museum
American Wing, Room 760

A disapproving docent in black blazer glares as I graph
Bierstadt's massive *The Rocky Mountains, Lander's Peak*
in my point-and-shoot way—snap, a step sideways, snap.
One square at a time, I rescue from dim prints and inadequate
    books
a dress's beadwork under braided hair, a tended kettle,
claws of a killed bear and faces rapt with a hunter's tale.
I hold the tiny camera above my head to level
the hero's peak, buff of clouds, glacier curving toward central falls.

I smile at the docent and he jerks his radio, hoping
for the shrill of the invisible barrier—*Sir, step back!*
Tall, broad-shouldered, more like a guard but nothing like
the petite, perfumed ancient stationed by the Monets,
he is tired of tour guides extolling the artist-explorer
and his satchel of sketches easeled into this grand compendium
of Indian life. He wants a story for the breakroom, a tale
of intervention and arrest. But I know my limit as I
hold breath, then release, over and over across this canvas
the size of thirty-seven opened coffee table books.
I am here for stories too, close enough now to walk
with the elk hunter's wife who dreams her hands
shaping soft hide to her husband's shoulders, to see
a dog guarding a cradled baby beside a tepee sketched
with seven bold-colored horses, to hear a man with carved pipe
teach his son the weight of smoke. So many stories they

start pushing and spill from the frame, dragging others
from behind, shouting and pointing: it's *Lander's* predecessor,
the lost pendant *Laramie Peak,* known only by reviews and a
    sidelong
gallery photograph, and here's Bierstadt himself, staging the painting

for a charity fair, big wigwam and natives drumming a Rattlesnake
        Dance;
he refuses ten thousand dollars and sells it for twenty-five
before it tours the States and Europe, and shrilling above them all
the seesawing critics, one gushing *Lander's Peak* is
"unexcelled by any landscape ever painted" and another grouching
"immature, and, on too pretentious a scale," and still

stories are pressing; they scramble this white room claiming
Lander's wall-mates—Church's *Heart of the Andes*
and General Washington being rowed—and now their stories too,
coil like jungle vines and river currents, stories swirling
to the ceiling and down to the floor, back to the feet
of the bored docent ready for his rotation to the Monets,
their simplicity and quiet, the way water lilies remind him
of the label on a bottle of scented oil, and how his wife
smiles as she stands dripping, toweling after her bath.

Sharon Presnell

Taproot

His name was I.C. What the "I" or the "C" stood for was pretty uncertain, best guess for "I" being "Irv". "C" was either some unknown middle name or his last name. The tall, willowy, man of few words was simply known as I.C. to his large Scotch-Irish Appalachian family and people around the small town in which they confined themselves. I suppose the bank would have known what the "I.C." stood for, except to anyone's recollection he never went there, preferring to do all of his business by cash or barter and burying his treasure in the ground around the property in large cans and jars that once held mass quantities of mayonnaise or beans used to feed the brood. They survived the depression by living on the land and a unique combination of ingenuity, minimalism, and will. When the depression ended, their insular way of life remained for the next two generations giving us great grandchildren of the 60's-70's a bizarre opportunity to live with one dusty boot planted in the 40's and one Nike sneaker headed toward the future. We know what it is like to live without electricity, cook food on a wood stove or outside in a big cauldron over a fire, frequent an outhouse, and use pulleys and buckets to lift the best water you've ever tasted up from deep in the ground and drink it straight out of a metal ladle. We know the sticky velvet of tobacco leaves in our hands and the sting of a saddleback worm in the corn field. We know the sweet smell of tobacco curing in the barn and the taste of red clay dust in our mouths. We know the feel of dirt packed tight under our nails while we pat the cool earth and beg the doodlebugs to come out and play.

There were a lot of us. I.C. was rumored to be one of 21 children, and each of those that survived had large families as well to make sure there were enough hands to run the farm. My aunt would frequently say you couldn't 'swing a cat' in Yadkin county without hitting a relative; as a literal child the expression confused me and I remember thinking 'poor cat' every time. Our circle was the smallest with only nine great grandchildren, but the family reunions brought together second and third cousins by the dozens until it was not possible to remember names or who belonged to who. The family genetics were powerful, with almost Marfan-like long arms, legs, and fingers, narrow hips and shoulders, long face and nose, and a slightly down-turned mouth that inverted only briefly for big smiles. My sister's children, now four generations beyond I.C., still bear many of those unique physical attributes.

My father's young life was absent toys and education but rich in work experience. None of the male kids of his generation finished school, their job was to work the farm and that was not challenged. The operation was substantial in his era; each day brought together his siblings, cousins, aunts, and uncles to plant, tend, harvest, cook, and feed to support the family. At the end of the day when the work was done everyone would retire to the primitive cabin nestled among the fields and barns. Women folk were serving up the evening meal of vegetables, cornbread, and beans or meat while a passel of children, ranging in age from 3-15, ran about. It's safe to picture 10-20 near-feral kids at any given time, darting in and out of the cabin, attempting to have some fun with home-made toys or farm pets.

Shortly after supper, old I.C. would shuffle off to the hanging barn where the tobacco was curing and pick out a few of the prettiest finished leaves and carry them back to the front porch where he assumed his position in an old straight-back wooden chair. He'd take those leaves and roll them up nice and tight. Then he would snip off some of that good home-grown stuff and mix it with cheap store-bought, get his chew going, and lean way back in the chair so the front legs were off the porch and the back rested on the side of the house. His head was tilted back and his eyes were closed, completely still except for the wiggle of his lower jaw working the tobacco. Kids ran around him, occasionally tempted to try and distract him with some hijinx but never quite brave enough. Every 20 minutes like clockwork, I.C. would startle and sit straight up, slamming the front legs of the chair back onto the porch with a bang. His eyes would fly open, and he would shout "SHIT FIRE!!" at the top of his lungs. After a brief pause he'd close his eyes and go right back to the lean, peaceful as anything, lower jaw quietly working the tobacco. All accounts suggest he wasn't yelling at the kids, or over anything in particular. It was probably some old Scotch-Irish Appalachia foothills form of meditation.

I was the first of my generation on that side of the family to get an education beyond high school, travel the world, or live in other states. Most of my life has been spent in limbo between the cocoon in which I was raised and my present existence with all its complexities and responsibilities. In my twenties I resented my upbringing for making me ignorant and not preparing me for the 'real world'. In my thirties as I became a mother I began to feel differently, to long for the opportunity to give my daughter the peace that comes with feeling the earth under your bare feet and hearing only the sounds of nature, free from the constant buzz of the information age. At 50-something I have come home to North Carolina and find indescribable comfort in the familiarity of it all. The farm is no longer operational, though the land remains in the family, for now at least. On a hot summer night if you walk down along the river and stay quiet, you just might hear old I.C. in the distance…"SHIT FIRE!"

Alan Elyshevitz

Insomnia, Part XIII

In some other time
       and country
             of four-sided
wind and minimal
       chromatics, every
             little thing
hosts a deity.
       Their hands
             are simple
threshers. They
       have returned
             to prior fabrics
and smoke
       their meats with
             original fuel.
They pulse
       without a
             pharmacy.
They have never
       known chambers of
             spackled walls
nor carbon
       monoxide detectors.
             They exult
in pleas
       of the glottis
             and suffer no
rhetorical deaths.
       They think
             the stars

into drama.
        Reclined on the
                softest clippings,
they sleep
        without noise
            in their skin.

John J. Hohn

Yankton County
1955

River Road, a dusty gravel vein,
stretches along the Missouri River basin.
Farmers and their families follow it
to the heart of town,
to shop and drink and pray.
Approaching Yankton,
it passes Sisters' Grove,
a dense stand of ash, elm, oak, and paper maple,
foreboding as celibacy,
dark as the convent itself.
Under its temple boughs,
chaste underbrush entangles
any presuming trespass.

The road rises in a slow rounding curve
from the river flood plain floor
to the convent grounds
where nuns can be seen
at any time of the year
gliding, heads down, in devotion
on the path of the stations of the cross,
their black habits flowing
like sails seeking home
in a backwater of sorrow.

The ancient Missouri,
a muddy, swirling current,
lies less than a mile distant.
On the opposite side, chalkstone bluffs,
steep palisades, bleached sunshine white,
form a high shimmering southern wall

to the gorge glacier-melt rutted
out of soft limestone
millennia before any human would stalk
along its banks.
The first to come upon the sentinel cliffs,
decided they were placed there
by a god beyond knowing.
The gash the melting torrent tore
through the prairie nourished the land
from the mountains of Montana to the Gulf.
Nearby, early explorers parlayed
with the Lakota and left a pox
upon their nation in parting,

Yankton became the last steamboat stop northward
on the inland artery of the continent,
a destination port where settlers,
emboldened by a sense of God-given entitlement,
disembarked and fanned out
across venerated prairie hunting grounds,
a human delta,
first ever, they'd declare,
to own a plot
of the virginal grassland.
With beast in harness,
they walked behind wooden-handled plows,
cleaving the primal sod,
laying it back and bare
like the entrails of slaughtered prey.

Emma Eisler

Verge

It is one of those spring nights where winter still nips at your fingers and toes, but the air smells of wildflowers. They are driving through a National Forest. To their right, the trees lean towards them, seeming to veer onto the road. To their left, there is the cliff's edge, the reservoir dancing magic below.

He, the boyfriend, is driving with a hand on her, the not-girlfriend's, thigh. They are taking turns swigging a bottle of whiskey. The windows are down so the moon kicks her feet back on the dash, coyotes howling along with radio static. Yes, the car is in the night, and the night is in the car, and the stars are playing tug of war with the wind in her hair.

She leans over the gearshift, kisses his neck and lets her hand dip to the fly of his jeans. "Would the Girlfriend do this?"

He turns to her, his smile a slant, and everything with the shimmering waves of being just past the line of too drunk, every flat surface in the world beginning to liquidate. "Let's not talk about Her."

"Why not? We're driving all night so you can see Her and you won't even acknowledge she exists?"

"Well, I'm here with you right now, aren't I?"

She leans back in her seat, crosses her arms over her chest. He can feel her wanting to speak, to bite back with something sharp, or equally to lean her head on his shoulder, close her eyes, and let her anger dissipate. He waits for her to decide, lets her squirm a moment longer.

She surprises him by turning towards the window. "I guess."

He chuckles slightly. She reminds him of a petulant little girl. He wishes she'd snap out of her sour mood so they could enjoy the night, but he also isn't one to press. No, he'll wait a while, see if she comes around.

The not-girlfriend was a friend of a friend, at first, loud at parties and brash, but always adjusting her shirt or dress, so he could tell her confidence was at best aspirational. He knows it is a point of tension for her that the Girlfriend is so thin. When he first met the not-girlfriend, she had a boyfriend. He'd see the two of them lazing in grassy knolls on campus, a soft strip of the not-girlfriend's pale skin showing in the space between her t-shirt and jeans. Her eyes seemed constantly to rove around. He wasn't drawn to her so much as vaguely curious. He felt she had the kind of body made awkward by the presence of clothes, and so he imagined her naked. She was noticeable in groups without being quite charming, her jokes verging at times on mean. He felt she would slurp any drop of affection like a cat to milk, and so he began to pay her attention.

The boyfriend takes another gulp of whiskey, then places the bottle down to let his hand trace down her back, his eyes still trained on the road. She turns to face him, her lips pursed in a way that should be unattractive but is made endearing by the barely suppressed longing she seems to contain each time she forgives him for some small infraction.

"Let's camp somewhere tonight," she says. "We can drive the rest of the way in the morning."

He smiles slightly. "You know I can't."

"We can leave before sunrise. You can just tell Her you got tired and needed a few hours sleep."

Something darts in front of the car and he grimaces, but whatever it is manages to escape without getting caught under the wheels, its eyes glowing amidst the brush. He was always a city boy until he graduated and moved out west. He can't get used to these endless dark roads between towns, all the creatures that skitter through the night.

She takes a drink. "What am I even doing here?"

"Enjoying my company, of course."

"Whatever."

She knows she should let go and just enjoy it, that this is what she gets – the space between these spread out towns and the way he threads his fingers through her hair, the pulsing, thumping *now* that not even the Girlfriend can take. But she can't shake the sullenness, the crinkle in her forehead and dissatisfaction in the fold of her arms. She can feel him thinking, *What exactly did you expect?* but she has no answer, save the sound of wind rustling the leaves of the canyon.

It didn't happen right away. There were a few drunken nights back in school, times the Girlfriend went home early or had other plans and never made it. He'd watch her from across the room, talk to groups of people closer and closer to her as the hours wore on, until suddenly he was beside her, laughing at her joke or just silently eyeing her as if waiting for her to finish. And then just as quickly he'd be gone into the cold air, or she'd leave thinking he'd walk out with her, only to watch him disappear back into the throng of the party. It happened the first time close to graduation, and then a few times just after, neither of them expecting it to continue. But then they both happened to move to the same far western state, separated only by a couple hour's drive. They weren't friends but saw each other under the pretense of friendship, undressing quickly in her barely furnished apartment over a bakery.

And then it was as if it had always been – him, driving through the night to see the Girlfriend in Her neighboring state, then driving past his own town to the not-girlfriend's and sleeping in her bed that smelled of frosting and mint soap. He shouldn't have let the not-girlfriend come with him this time, a foolish and, if we're honest, somewhat demeaning plan – dropping her off at a hotel, so he can stop at the 24-hour supermarket and buy flowers, then wrap the Girlfriend in his arms.

The car veers over the yellow line, and he considers that he should possibly slow down on the whiskey. She notices and leans over the center console, says in a nasally tone he thinks is probably mocking, "I thought you had it all together."

He grips the wheel a little tighter. "I'm fine."

She reaches out to stroke the line of his jaw. "I'd die with you, if you asked. I'd go headfirst into the reservoir. Would She?"

He can picture it all too clearly, the windows filling up with icy water, moonlight spilling over the metal as it sinks. He veers towards the edge. "Let's go, then." For a second, the tires graze open air. She braces for impact. But then they are back in the correct lane going forward. She looks over him and squints, trying to make out the distance of the reservoir below. No light. So different from the east where everything is illuminated by buildings or passing cars.

She knows that, for him, this kind of open landscape makes him feel small or lonely, disjointed without the comforts and background noise of a college campus or city. For her, though, this land is one of possibility – where on solitary highways, he can be hers and she can be no one's at all, can pass on into the next world with little sound or ceremony.

"You wouldn't," she says. "But I would."

He laughs slightly, takes another sip of whiskey, though he senses he should know better. "You're so dark sometimes." He sees it in the way she fucks, pupils wide and head rolled back like she wants to be dissolved in him, then all at once, coming awake and clinging onto him with such ferocity, nails dug into his back, so it seems she wants to occupy his very skin, to pull him into her or put herself in him so completely that there cannot be room in his heart for anyone else.

She barks out a laugh. "So, what? You don't want to die with me?"

He glances out the window. "Can we talk about something else?"

"What flowers are you going to buy Her?" she asks. "Will you fuck on the couch or can you make it to the bed?"

"You're not funny," he replies.

"Can't we just pull over and sleep somewhere? Just for a little while."

Emma Eisler **107**

He keeps driving. "I said I'd get in tonight."

She reaches for the steering wheel and tries to turn it. "Come on, please."

He thrusts her hands away. "The hell are you doing."

She pouts. "I'm sorry. I was kidding. I just want to spend time with you."

Once, they were driving through the dark after a camping trip he wanted to go on based on some idealized vision of exploring the west he'd grown up on, and they decided to stop at a rest stop. He placed his hand on the small of her back and led her inside. She felt so lovely under the fluorescent gas station lights, leaves still tangled in her hair. He went down a separate aisle to grab a couple beers, while she picked out snacks. They both happened to look up from across the store at the same time, and he smiled at her in such a way that she could imagine for a moment how it would feel to be loved by him, to walk through town holding hands or open the door to find him with outstretched bouquet. She couldn't tell if the knot in her stomach was disgust or desire.

For the millionth time, he considers telling her they should probably stop whatever it is they're doing. He pulls over to the shoulder. "Let's not fight, okay?"

She nods and leans into him. Her breath smells of whiskey and mint, him of a vaguely cheesy aftershave she found off-putting at first, but now associates so deeply with him that she knows she'll miss it on the hotel pillow when he drops her off. They kiss for a while, his hands running through her hair, teasing along her spine and between her legs. She feels the moment sliding already away from her, a car winding around a turn, spring boiling over into summer heat and then cooling again to fall.

She has trained her body so well to desire these in-betweens, all the nowhere towns where he lets himself want her. She could be a ghost, could disappear so easily between here and there. Once, they met at the shore of a lake, rolled in the sand so the water lapped at their feet, and it took days to wash the grit from her hair, and she burned her tongue holding back everything she wanted to say, kissed him without leaving a mark but imagined her lips leaving blooms like matches.

Where does this end? she wants to ask. *Do I move into a little house down the street from yours after you get married? Tuck a key under my doormat so you can find me in bed after the Girlfriend—now Wife—falls asleep?*

He leans over her and pushes back her seat, slings his body over the gearshift to climb atop her. She eases down her pants, ignores the moonglow of her naked skin and tries not to picture how the Girlfriend must look when She is the one with him. The not-girlfriend's breathing grows disconnected and high, her own moans reverberating in her ears, and there is such an ugliness to this intimacy, this clumsy body she lives in with all of its animal longings, but none of that matters – prettiness isn't her domain.

After it's over, he slides back into the driver's seat and they pull onto the road in silence. She will not bother asking again to camp for the night, now that they've both had a version of what they wanted. She feels her drunkenness begin to wear off and takes another sip. He watches her tug on her jeans, suck in her stomach to pull the zipper. Sometimes he almost loves her, but always there is something so fearsome about her, bristling and unwilling to accept this kind of intimacy. He thinks they both wish it could be otherwise, or maybe this is delusional – he knows what she thinks, that he's never going to leave the Girlfriend anyway, no matter what he whispers in her ear some nights.

He keeps his hands steady on the wheel, and eventually they are through the canyon and passing again the dim lights of old mining towns, neon gas stations and Super 8s. He allows himself to feel some relief; soon they will be in the town where the Girlfriend lives, and the not-girlfriend will be tucked away in a hotel. He will go to the store and buy flowers, and in Her arms, the tightness in his gut will soon dissipate. The car will not hit a coyote or hare; there will be no blood tonight, and no one will sink in opaque depths of water. He allows himself to smile, his hand to graze the not-girlfriend's knee.

The not-girlfriend asks, "Where would you go tonight, if you could go anywhere?"

She imagines him arriving at the Girlfriend's home. How pretty She will look in the gentle light of lampposts, arched back and arms looped around his neck. And the not-girlfriend knows she has always been an apparition on the tarmac of their love, a phantom presence in each room of their present and future houses, but if he can only give her the right answer, then she will accept those terms.

He replies at last, "I'd go and go and never get there."

Sharon Louise Howard

Sanity Quilt

they do everything together away from home:
grocery shopping, drug store, doctor visits—even
the small town library every other week:
he likes to know what she reads

needing to keep her hands busy, her mind occupied:
she gathers the worn out old discarded
anything material no longer needed
wanted or torn or outdated or hated
cuts into approximation of squares
needle & thread in hand tv on half-listening
those characters what did they know of the real world
in tin-can home mid-atlantic mid-summer
middle of empty countryside with air conditioner out
windows paint-stuck shut, he won't fix:

best left, he says, *harder to open from outside*
anything happens to you would kill me, he says
how can she argue with that

she pieces together haphazard patches:
faded denim against cotton, satin against wool
the uglier the juxtapositions the better:
sheets, jeans, shirts, skirts
rubbed-thin towels—the miniature light
flannel blanket never used, that pale
forget-me-not blue—she had not forgotten
the one piece she has not yet cut into
her hands shake when she tries
she wraps ice in the tiny blanket
places it between her neck and the sofa back
closes her eyes imagines anything anyplace different

stuck home—remote—months gone by
full four by six feet of abstract distraction complete
mid-autumn with winter looming—the night
she knew would come:

don't wait dinner, he says, *don't wait up*
he won't be home till morning or later

sun long ago gone down
mid-bed she spreads the misshapen quilt
lights the matches one by one
till the patches catch and hold the flame
she snatches up a small case packed
with few clothes toothbrush snacks for the road
a map of the first large city north torn
from a library book
& the folded blue blanket
she walks out
swaddled into the night

Emily Carter

Reset

Control Alt Delete
She wrote
Big letters
On the mirror
On the pad in the kitchen
On a hot pink sticky note
Positioned over the odometer
Pushing reset
On life

She broke up with her
Hairdresser
Pastor
Housekeeper
Counselor
Tennis pro
Accountant
Financial planner
Keeping the quiet man who mowed grass in perfect lines
Because that's so hard to find

She reasoned it was time for a change
Mix it up a bit
Shake things down
Step outside the box
Saying it was her and not them
But she would have kept on
Pacing with the Joneses
They had moved ahead now triumphant

She checked the box marked single
Party of one
She wrote Jesus as her emergency contact
But only she saw the humor
Which was okay
Laughing still counts as laughing
Even when alone

Susan Bavaria

Chrysalis

Transformation isn't sweet and bright. It's a dark and murky painful pushing.
Victoria Erickson

Throughout elementary school, Eve contracts no flu, colds, sore throats or earaches, her un-coddled immune system burned tough by neglect. Her teeth are perfectly straight, "as if she's worn braces for a year," says the dentist. But there's always the undercurrent, that she is not normal despite impeccable sonatinas at piano recitals, her poise with adults, the handshake-to-impress I teach her from a newsletter about international business. Her plusses tethered to a dark twin -- talent and unworthiness, compassion and anger. She learns how to negotiate life with her invisible handicap. Only we parents see her demons

"How is our little Boccalina today?" my husband Paul asks as if he's checking the weather. We're careful not to use the feminine version of the Italian word for "mouth" in her presence. She slams her bedroom door so often that the paint on the doorjamb flakes.

As I look back over the three years of Eve's acting out her rage before we finally put her in a lockdown adolescent treatment center, it seems that anger, or a form of it, is constant in our lives. It escalates gradually so we adapt, like a frog placed in cold water that eventually boils to death.

* * *

"I want you to feel comfortable," I tell Eve. "They have a dress code at Island View. Let's go to Express and get you a few things."

Her mood isn't edgy, no "what the hell's up your ass?" which makes me grateful. The mall feels cool. I sit on the corner of a display block bearing stacks of cropped T-shirts in lemon, mango and other fruit smoothie colors.

"You can't show any skin," I say. She scowls. "Around the midriff, it's one of the rules." My words trail behind her back to the dressing room.

The weekend before she leaves for treatment, I watch her nap. Asleep in a T-shirt and capri pants, she looks vulnerable and sweet, thin youthful limbs, bare feet. She doesn't look like one of 20 percent of children between 12 and 14 who've had sex.

I hear her one-sided phone conversation.

"Top or bottom?"

"Get him liquored up first. Aaron had so much scotch one night he couldn't ride his bicycle."

"Take liquor from the back of the cabinet where they won't see it."

"Do you have any weed? Grass. Not that alfalfa shit."

"Listen to this. It's from the Internet. 'Semen is pure and sterile. It's insulting if you spit it out.'" I decide not to burden Paul with this information.

Her temper and volatility have caused us to lock sharp knives and liquor in the garage and pack our favorite pieces of Santa Clara pottery in a closet. She is too unpredictable. We grab a precious half-hour of quiet at the coffee shop only when she sleeps in on Saturday morning. It's the way we must live now, wary, trapped, embarrassed to tell anyone that when she says "Fuck you, dumb butt!" we mumble and move away.

"She's so committed to opposing you and Paul, I think it's probably best for her to go away for treatment," says her psychiatrist.

"Are you trying to get rid of me?" Eve asks when I tell her.

"No, no," I say in two octaves. "We want to help you."

"Where are all the cosmetic bags?" her voice shrill the morning she leaves. I scurry and find two. Paul and I have barely slept. He sat in a chair on the back patio facing her window for half the night, but she hasn't run.

I pulverize the French roast coffee beans, one-one thousand, two-two thousand, make an effort to find Paul's favorite *No tabac made a man of me* mug, pour in milk and heat it in the microwave before pouring in coffee so it's hot the way he likes it.

"Move." Eve elbows me aside in the hallway. I glare at her.

"What!" she says.

"I'm not even in your way."

Eve's stepsister Suzy arrives, perky, positive, a physical therapist accustomed to reassuring anxious people.

"Hi Evie, can I help you get ready?" They disappear into her bedroom. At Eve's request, Paul's 34-year-old daughter will accompany Eve to Island View Residential Treatment Center outside Salt Lake City. No extraction by professional handlers needed.

After a half-hour ride to the airport, Eve gets out and turns to my window. "Stay out of my bedroom."

"Okay." I almost laugh out loud at her absurd request. We can't wait to tackle the underpants balled up under the bed with so much dust you barely see the color. Towels dot the floor. A dirty window screen lay under the bed, popped out so often for her midnight runs to meet someone at the park down the street that the rim is bent. A piece of lined paper on her bulletin board reads "Lazy chicks don't like to fuck." I never understand what that means.

I watch an automatic door close behind her rolling suitcase.

"Do you think I should go in?"

"Susan," Paul lifts his hands from the steering wheel palms up, a supplicant to the patron saint of beleaguered parents. "Just go."

Eve turns her back to me at the ticket counter. I hug Suzy and whisper "Thank you so much. Call us tonight when you get back."

Paul waits at curbside. I get in the car. He pulls away and we look at each other as slow smiles creep across our faces. Nothing needs saying. It's like some cheesy movie finale where the music crescendos as Paul drives west. Snow covered peaks of the Rocky Mountains extend north and south as far as we can see. Jets become silver specks in the sky. Fresh greenery hides deer in the wetlands along the airport road. Everywhere I look, possibility emanates. Paul and I are two horses unyoked from the plow to frolic in the pasture.

"Now we can get on with our lives…we can actually have a life that doesn't revolve around Eve," I say.

"She's gone. I'm so relieved," says Paul, giving the steering wheel a high five. "I was sure she'd try to run away last night."

I savor my first day free from Eve. I rent the movie *Gods and Monsters* and check out eight self-help books from the library, including one on fasting, then can't resist buying an ice cream cone with coconut, dark chocolate and almonds. I remove sticky Dr. Pepper from kitchen walls with Murphy's Oil soap, and scrub baseboard and floor with a hardwood cleaner. I lie on the couch and gaze out at our silver maple tree through the glass sliding doors, green and fresh.

We pick Suzy up at the airport that evening. She tells us of driving around Park City, eating lunch, putting off the inevitable check-in and strip search.

"It's a nice place," she reassures us. She hands me a bag with chunky soled shoes, shorts, tops with spaghetti straps. "Eve had too many clothes." I wonder how Eve felt having watched Suzy walk through doors that shut and lock, unsure when she'll see any of us again.

"I met her therapist, Robert Wilde. He's kind of quiet. I hope Eve doesn't manipulate him. He's going to call you at 2:30 tomorrow."

The next day, at 2:20, I sit at Paul's big oak desk and wait. At 2:23 I pick up the receiver and make sure there's a dial tone. I have a legal pad in front of me. I test the pen. I wait.

June 1. Perfect posture. Edge of couch. Lighten up. Pretty uptight. Not fully open. I write phrases on a yellow legal pad, trying to keep up with Robert's conversation.

"She started to talk about her biological family. She drew a modified family tree on a wipe board," he says. He asks me to photocopy pages from two photo albums Eve brought when we adopted her from social services six years ago, photos of Aunt Lois and Uncle Buddy, her sisters, Stacy, Star and Penny, brothers Evan and Quentin, biological parents Donald and Shirley.

Tearful off and on. Angry about that. Likes to be in control. Girls reaching out to her.

"She says she won't be defiant and agrees that rules are good."

Silver team. 19 girls. Positive peer culture. Fosters openness. Family therapy–2 p.m. Tuesday afternoon by phone. Two tactics kids use to get their parents to take them out. "This place isn't doing anything" or "It's awful."

"Does she need to actually say what happened to her? Before she can get better?" I ask. The secret things she's never spoken to me. What she remembers about her biological father and Uncle Leroy? Why she hates stuffed animals? Why clowns are scary? Why I must close her closet door tightly before she goes to bed even at age 14? Can these be exposed, like a vampire to the sun, seared to ashes, harmless wisps to blow away, never to damage again?

"I don't know," says Robert. "It will get worse before it gets better. Don't be discouraged or feel like you're wasting money. You know, sometimes it's best to send kids to boarding school after they leave here so they won't be tempted with old behavior."

"Of course, we expect her to get well, to come home," I say, willing this hostile alternative away.

"It was such a heartbreaking decision for you to send her away," says Paul's cousin at a family picnic. No, it wasn't, not really. People treat me like I'm fragile and have endured a great loss, but what I feel is not grief but relief.

Eve is a Newcomer in the Island View status system, the first level assigned to every new resident. She wears a colored woven bracelet of purple and green that designates her rank and must wait two weeks to get to the next level, which is Compliance. Every Friday her Silver Team goes on field trips, and the first one is to a greenhouse where the girls choose a plant that represents them.

"I picked an aloe vera, Mom," she says on a phone call. "Tough on the outside, smooth inside."

Her summer session classes are canoe making, astronomy and career choices. She's in a chemical dependency group "because," Robert says, "sexual abuse correlates highly with substance abuse."

Each girl on her team performs an assigned task that's rotated every few weeks. "Rooster" wakes the girls up. "Compass" explains rules. "Sherlock" scrutinizes for clothing violations. Eve is the "Beautician." She unlocks the Silver Team beauty box twice a day and checks out restricted items like mirrors, tweezers and nail polish remover.

She goes everywhere with the Silver Team, one of three girls' peer groups. She is structured, therapized and watched 24/7, an insect pinned on a wax tray. She cannot escape the scrutiny, the microscope, what she says, how, and to whom she says it. My role as parent feels non-existent now. She has a recreational therapist, a team therapist, an individual therapist, a psychiatrist. Even the teachers report back on her attitude and state of mind. It's all part of her "milieu."

I'm anxious to see the movie *Happiness* because it's about pedophilia. I tuck a small tablet and pen in my purse when I go, so certain am I about gaining an insight into Eve that I'm sure I'll need to take notes in the dark. However, I come out of the theater, and the tablet is still blank.

A movie can't grapple with the unwieldy, convoluted nature of child abuse and its long-term aftermath. *Happiness* is too much cause and effect, "if this, then that," all variables neatly packed like a box of Harry and David fruit. It seems to show equal empathy for the pedophile and has a linear plot: Man – Son – Son's friend – Sleepover – Drug Son's friend – Disclosure – Pariah in community – Divorce.

The neuropsychology of a pedophile's relationship with a young victim begins subtly. Secret touching, verbal intimidation, confusion, lies, an amalgam of feeling good and feeling guilty. How do you show how the scariness seeps into synapses, subtly, daily, changing the way a brain reacts to the world, molding it to be more irritable, impulsive, and hypervigilant? How do you chronicle that?

Eve's view of the world cannot be explained with a pat answer. Nor can it be totally healed. "Early childhood stress isn't something you 'get over' says Dr. Martin Teicher, MD, PhD, associate professor at Harvard Medical School. Eve's symptoms may be the result of abuse, but more aggravated problems such as major depression, borderline personality and impulse disorders could emerge when she's older.

Eve reminds me of a succulent plant that Paul had when we got married. It formed an upright, leathery green pod one year that eventually opened into a strange, exotic flower with five dark purple and chartreuse rays. Lurid and sensual, it existed to catch the attention of a passing pollinator. Later that week I noticed a bad smell in the room like rotting meat or garbage. Sniffing, I discovered its source was the flower, a stapelia, also known as carrion flower, pollinated by flies. Eve's damaged core, I fear, will only attract what is terrible.

I check and double-check our phones to make sure they work. Eve can call between 6:30 and 8:00 p.m. for five minutes on Thursday, a new privilege. Paul waters his hanging baskets. "You better go in," he tells me at 6:37 even though we could probably hear the phone through the screen. She is number 00512-31, a number I must tell the caller. I can't talk to her without it.

"They say I may be here longer than the summer." She's testy.

"We believe in the program. Whatever the therapists say is what we'll do."

"That's so unfair. What if my friends aren't there when I get out? I'm supposed to start high school!"

"I think you need to engage with the treatment, Eve. You need to open up and talk. If you don't do that, it will take longer." I don't say that I think she needs a whole bunch of new friends.

"The girls say I front," a term from group therapy that means she masks what she's feeling. "You can't trust people. They take what you say and turn it around. These girls are bitches."

"Remember what your psychiatrist said? That you needed to work on growing a longer fuse?" There is a pause. Then she voices the sorrow that runs as a theme throughout her life, the fear at the bottom of her fury.

"If I had a longer fuse, everyone would run over me."

I wish the sun would take a vacation
Leave me in darkness for awhile
Let me heal
Let me try to figure out why I'm fucked up
Henry Rollins

Les Brown

Aunt Sarah Hula Hoops

She's swinging her hips in circles,
keeps the Hula Hoop riding in orbits.
Her short gray hair shining in noon sun,
bright as the smile on her wrinkled round face.
Her floured apron wafts in the breeze.
She has no reason for joy.
Her father had beaten out
her unborn passion child.
Still she cannot be bent to his will
on the crumb of land thrown to her
like a scrap from his laden table.
She laughs, and sips family bourbon,
keeps the rhythm of life moving
above the earth in which he lies.

Sandra Dreis

Jeppi - 1984

Stages dark on Mondays, Jeppi foiled my hair.
My Siamese, Izzy, assuming the silver squares
were his birthright, honed skills as a burglar.

Aside from theatre, Jeppi adored three things:
lover Michael, dog Muffy, salty gossip.
Thus, my naive self gazed secondhand at gay

nightlife in Manhattan's West Village. Sites for casual
sex abounded. Filthy subway bathrooms, the Rambles
in Central Park, Christopher Street bars and dives.

Darker practices, S & M hangouts, anonymous
sex clubs. Drug-infused orgies in the Pines
and Cherry Grove, common knowledge on Fire Island.

I kiboshed further details. Served Jeppi killer coffee
instead. Chat veered off into OCD stage managers,
zombie audiences, but returned to dying young men.

First time I heard the word, *AIDS,* was summer,
spoken by a beautiful man in his twenties, shouldering
a bulky dance bag at 50th, the crosstown bus stop.

Michael got sick first; after the funeral, living in terror,
Jeppi followed. Thin as bone, he sought home,
Fairfax County, Virginia—taken in by an old high school

friend when scandalized parents turned him away.
His final goodbye came late one night. He laughed,
snorted actually, when I described Izzy's successful

pounce on a lemon meringue pie. We felt okay, then.
Like sharing a slice. Muffy, his loyal mutt, mourned
beneath my desk, twice adopted, twice adored.

Howard Pearre

Oki Joe's Decision

The patrol car flashed its blue lights and pulled alongside the concrete median. A short, commanding "woo-oop" of its siren made sure everyone paid attention. Traffic eased through the intersection. Drivers peered at the commotion.

"Where's your ID, Joe?"

Oki Joe shifted his cardboard sign, reached into a pocket of his Army jacket, and pulled out a dirty laminated card.

"My chain broke."

"Well, if you're going to be out here, you've got to display it."

"I gotta get another chain," Joe said.

"I guess so," said the officer. "Until then, you're gonna have to hold it so it can be seen, or you'll have to get off the street. Don't let me come by again and not see it." The officer handed Joe a dollar.

"Too hot out here anyway. Thanks."

It had been one of those August days like when he'd arrived in Okinawa three decades ago. Exiting the Pan Am 727 into the humidity after an eighteen-hour air conditioned ride from Travis, he felt like he'd stepped into a sauna. It was 6 a.m., and he had eighteen months to go.

Not only was his ID chain broken, his sign was torn. He'd folded it over and used it as a pillow the night before instead of rolling up his extra shirt. He'd given the shirt to Sally Alley because hers was so worn it was starting to look obscene, not much more than a rag that wasn't fit to cover a woman regardless of how she made her way in life. And because he'd bent it over twice, it had torn along a crease, and the word "VETERAN," printed in Magic Marker ink, was barely readable. Now he'd have to find another chain as well as some cardboard. To complicate matters, Crazy Ike, who had the Magic Marker, had gone to Virginia where he said he hoped to stay with his daughter for a while.

Finding cardboard would be easy. There were dumpsters behind the mall a short distance from the group's encampment in the patch of trees a dozen yards from the whizzing cars where, so far, nobody had thought of a store to put up. But making the cardboard into a sign without Ike's marker would be a challenge.

Joe waited for a red light, crossed three lanes, and headed for the little camp—several lean-tos, Sally's light blue nylon tent, and a couple of grocery carts. Later, he paid a visit to the dumpster behind Circuit City. When he returned with fresh cardboard, he borrowed Sally's ballpoint pen and block-printed the words "VIET VET." It wasn't as clean as a marker job, but the cardboard wasn't bent. It also wasn't exactly the truth. While the shooting was going on "down south," he'd been assigned to motor pool duty on Okinawa, the temporary home of thousands of servicemen and women of all brands. Just creative marketing, Joe rationalized.

The next morning, Joe pulled a bag of saltines from his backpack for breakfast and made his way through the brush and trees to the edge of the street. Shielding his eyes from the sun rising above the Home Depot store, he was surprised, and confused, by what he saw: a large man, a *very* large man with a beard even scruffier than his, flying a sign on the concrete median.

Not cool, Joe thought. That was *his* spot. It had been his since he'd joined the group at Ike's invitation after they met at a VA clinic. Joe had asked if anyone else was working the median, and no one was.

But who was *this* guy?

"Well, lookie there," said Ratty Ray. "He sure is big!"

Joe couldn't tell if Ray was trying to report information that was obvious or just getting in a dig, thankful that the stranger wasn't occupying *his* corner. Of course, the man might show up at Ray's spot tomorrow.

"Where'd he come from?" said Ray.

"Search me," said Joe. That was the thing. People just showed up. Sometimes they never said a word. Sometimes they'd get chatty with anybody who wouldn't walk away. The next day, they were gone, like they'd never been there.

Joe fumed and went back to the camp. From time to time during the day he walked over to the street to keep an eye on the median and the stranger. As he watched, every ten minutes or so someone would roll down a window and pass over a bill or some coins.

The man never smiled. As far as Joe could tell, he never even said or mouthed a thank-you. He just stuffed the money into a dirty pocket and shuffled to the next car. Then, when the light changed and the cars started moving, he'd make his way back along the median to the intersection.

About four o'clock, Joe watched as the man waited for the light to change, crossed the street, and left. He never spoke to the others, never looked up at them.

Must be heading for the shelter, Joe thought, scrambling back to the camp to find his own sign. When the light turned red, he hustled through the cars to the median. He tried to make eye contact with the first driver, but the man stared straight ahead. He moved to the next car, then to the next.

At the end of the day, Joe had collected four dollars and some change. He headed back to the little camp. Later, he crossed the street to a Burger King and bought a fish sandwich to go with the rest of the crackers for supper.

After some discussion with the others about the stranger who'd helped himself to the median, Joe settled into his lean-to. A large piece of cardboard atop several smaller pieces served as a bed. He stretched his jacket over the top of his body and formed one of its arms into a pillow, making himself as comfortable as he could.

When sleep came, the dreams came, too, as they often did since that Saturday night in Okinawa. Several soldiers were hanging around the barracks since they were out of spending cash. Another soldier, who Joe did not know, barged in waving an Army-issue .45

he'd somehow gotten his hands on. He screamed incoherently, stumbled, and fell to the floor a few feet from two soldiers who were playing cards on a bunk. The pistol, jarred from his hand, scooted away. But before anyone could react, he scrambled, grabbed it, aimed, and shot the two card-players. Seconds later he noticed Joe and the other man. He pointed the gun at Joe, glared at him, but then shoved it under his own chin and fired. Joe and the others in the barracks were unharmed, but the man's face, his scramble to retrieve the weapon, the blasts, the two soldiers falling to the floor, the hand of one twitching for moments before he lay still, and the shooter's horrible death was a scene Joe had never been able to put out of his mind. It was over in less than a minute, but in his dreams it replayed and replayed, always in slow-motion. This time a blurry image of the bearded stranger was the shooter. Joe awoke in a sweat two hours before dawn. He sat on the cardboard, letting the dreams fade and listening to the sporadic morning traffic.

As the others spread out to their spots, Joe worried about the intruder. But when he got to the edge of the little grove, he saw the median was empty. He crossed through the traffic, and took up his position. He'd picked up a piece of twine near the dumpster and now was legal with his ID showing.

The day was just as hot as the previous one, but Joe wore his Army jacket anyway, both to enhance his image as a veteran and to make sure nobody took it. That was the other thing. People would share food or cigarettes or even a blanket if you found yourself without, but they'd also steal anything you left lying around. You had to pay attention.

He finished the day with twelve dollars and change. He had bought a McDonald's cheeseburger for lunch and two more for supper. Sally and Ray left early. Ray had a grocery cart that the two piled all their possessions onto and said they were going somewhere else in the city for a while. Joe knew "a while" might be a long time.

The following morning, Joe woke up to find cooler weather, clouds, and drizzle. The jacket would feel good, and the drizzle would help in another way. While rain made you look pathetic and, therefore, was good for business, it also kept the car windows up. But with a light drizzle, drivers seemed more willing to lower their windows and open their wallets. He ate the rest of his crackers and made his way to the street.

At that moment, Joe spotted the big man, not on the median, but standing at the side of the road near the intersection. As before, he just stood, flying his sign and staring at drivers.

Then Joe took in the rest of the scene. Several feet behind the man, a skinny woman and two young children, all with blank expressions, sat huddled on a dirty yellow blanket under a golf-style umbrella next to several bulging black plastic bags and a Playmate cooler. The woman wore blue jeans and a Mickey Mouse sweatshirt. One child, slightly older than a baby, Joe calculated, wore a dirty tee shirt, diapers, and no shoes. The other child also was shoeless and wore shorts and a pink jacket.

Joe's feelings spun—from being incensed at how the big man had appropriated his spot the previous day, to pity, to disgust at how he was exploiting his wife and children, to admiring his cleverness for the same, and finally almost to respecting him, understanding he was doing what he had to do to take care of his family.

During the morning, Joe watched the man collect bill after bill. Once, the woman stood, conferred with the man, and took the children across the highway to the McDonalds. They emerged twenty minutes later with no evidence of a purchase, returned, and settled again.

About noon the drizzle cleared, and the sun came out. The man took a break, walked to the McDonalds, and returned with two bags. The family sat on their blanket and had a picnic within sight of the Home Depot, Burger King, McDonalds, a Toys-R-Us, and a carpet store. Other than eating their lunch, the woman and children did nothing but sit.

Late in the afternoon, with business slow, Joe crossed the highway and headed for the McDonalds, planning to invest in an afternoon cheeseburger. As he walked though the parking lot, he had to side-step some trash on the pavement. He looked at the wadded-up bag with napkins stuffed inside, a half-eaten hamburger, and a cardboard container with a few French fries. He considered retrieving the burger rather than expending his own funds, but, flush with his take so far, he dismissed the idea. He shook his head in disgust at the laziness of whoever had thrown it on the ground rather than taking it just ten feet to a trash container.

Joe reached down and picked up the paper items, but not the food—the birds would take care of that. Careful to avoid the smeared ketchup, he walked toward the trashcan. As he pushed in the metal flap, he noticed something green hidden behind the napkins, a detail that did not fit with the McDonalds brand color scheme. He examined the trash more closely. Peeking from behind a crumpled napkin was a bill—United States currency!

Joe quickly extracted his prize and discovered it included an oval portrait of President Ulysses Grant—a fifty! For a long moment he looked around the parking lot, expecting, but hoping not, to see the rightful owner speed-walking toward him. But no one came. A feeling of elation surged through his body.

He glanced across the highway to a Citgo station with a prominent "LOTTO!" sign and knew immediately how he would use his windfall. The promise of a bonanza scratch-off win took total control of his thoughts. He let the trash drop to the ground. He forgot about the afternoon snack.

Joe didn't wait for a light to change to cross the six lanes. Holding the fifty-dollar bill tight in his fist, he rushed through the traffic, waving to drivers to let him pass. He reached the other side of the highway, rushed by a car at a gas pump, and glanced back across the road. Seeing the big man with his sign and the woman and children on the blanket, he stopped suddenly, his mind a tangle of feelings

For all the years he'd been on the street, stood on corners and medians with cardboard signs, and slept in crowded shelters and in the little camps, he'd never seen a sight as pathetic as the little family sitting on the blanket. He knew many of the men and women who stood on curbs begging with their eyes for drivers to roll down their car windows were fathers and mothers, and that, as often as not, those crude signs saying "need help to feed my kids" weren't fake.

The driver of the car finished pumping gas, got into his car, and started the motor. The sound startled Joe. He walked toward the street, debating himself.

When the traffic stopped for a red light, Joe crossed the road and approached the family. The big man watched, glaring a warning. Without a word and without ever consciously deciding, Joe reached out to the woman and offered her the fifty. Without speaking or changing her expression, the woman looked at him, reached up, and took it. The large man's expression never changed.

Joe turned, crossed the road, and walked back to the little camp. He needed to think about what he'd done.

Alan Elyshevitz

Stanch

I am wary of blood
        unlike a boxer's cornerman
               or a prep cook
for a casino
        with bad odds
               where paper towels
dab extremis
        Men of my lineage
               live in containers
that predict their
        own leakage
               When a storm
each fall sends water
        through the walls
               we make stilts
for wired appliances
        and hold the family
               photos high
Bodily fluids
        defile creatures
               subject to seepage
that tend to have
        cuticles and brains
               of moderate size
My good dog
        died who is no
               "it" in my mind
Blood in his mouth
        told the time despite
               many rags
to choose from
        that wind and bind
               I know we are

bladders instead
    of insects
        Love resides
in a bare hand's
      pressure on terminal
       distress

Mark Caskie

Gregory Brockton, 1932

Depression-tough, you held on to your
job at the mill despite the long
hours, the low wages, the shanty
on the outskirts or Milton.
Your whitewalled Model-T
just edges into the picture,
the one you kept running
by scouring junk yards
and once even stripping
the wiring out of the wall
of your shack. In the foreground,
you squat, right arm around
your collie, Buster, who looks
skittishly at the camera,
as if he was used to having
stones thrown at him before
you took him in. In your
left hand, a thin white
cigarette held scoop fashion,
put out just long enough
for your brother to take
the picture he insisted
on taking on his visit
up from Pennsylvania.
You're quite serious in this photo,
a man who is willing to stay
in one place and to work
for his wages.

There is another picture,
Buster sits on the hood
of your Model-T, his tongue out, ears
perked, eager for one of the rides

you used to take him on,
the two of you, driving country lanes,
spinning your dust into oblivion.

Angela La Voie

The Icehouse

The winter I was seven, my father built me an igloo in our New Jersey backyard after a blizzard. To start, he traced a circle in the snow. He cut down part of his first row of snowy bricks so that he could work in a spiral. Each successive row leaned closer to the center than the one before it. At the top of the dome, he left a small empty ring for ventilation.

"If you build an igloo right, you can even build a fire inside," he said. How Dad knew about igloo construction, I didn't know. A math major in college, his mind was full of stray facts like baseball stats and how many pounds champion weightlifters could press.

When the bricks were in place, he used handfuls of snow as mortar between the rows, which he said gave further strength to the structure. Dad was six foot two, the igloo a little taller. The uneven mortar marred the igloo's geometric beauty only slightly.

Alone, I stood at the igloo's center, my father outside. I peered at the sky through the hollow center of the dome. The powder white skies under which Dad had labored had yielded to the sun. A bright blue dot of sky hailed the greater world. Pink and yellow sunlight streamed through the cracks of the bricks near the top of the roof, where Dad hadn't reinforced them. For a moment, all I could hear was quiet. The cold leached through my plastic snow boots. But the air was warmer inside the igloo than outside. The cold lingered only in my feet. I felt sheltered, safe.

The silence was interrupted by the sound of Mom wrestling open my bedroom window and then by her voice. "The driveway still needs to be shoveled. And I don't want Angela inside that icehouse. It could collapse on her," she called.

"Angela. Where are you?" she said in a louder voice. There was no escaping Mom's command. I took a moment longer to gaze at the rainbow halos of light.

"Come where I can see you!" she said. I brought myself to stand at the igloo's entrance.

"I don't want you going inside again. You could get hurt. Now come into the house for breakfast."

I looked once more through the doorway, hoping to steal a farewell before leaving my father's glorious creation. Mom remained at the window, though, watching until I passed her view, on my way to the front porch. I felt guilty that I wanted to stay outside with Dad when Mom wanted me in the house with her. Minutes later, the warmth of the kitchen embraced me. Mom fixed me a plate of pancakes. She made one in the shape of a snowman.

Dad's structure held about a week, until the sun's rays and rising temperatures reduced it to a low ruin. Even at that age, I understood what Mom meant about the driveway needing to be shoveled. Family tasks were not always top of mind for Dad.

Sometimes, at night, Mom would lift me from bed and pull sleepy arms through the sleeves of my coat. Then she would bundle me in blankets in the backseat of her Chevy station wagon. We would go out looking for Dad. Occasionally, on turns, my blankets would slip across the vinyl bench seat, causing me to shift. Sometimes my cheek would find its way to the cold vinyl. If I was too stirred to sleep, I learned to look for the white sodium glare of the streetlights. Their prevalence and distance from each other told me where we were headed, out along Route 1, Route 18, or the side streets. Mom checked for Dad at motel offices, taverns, and the bars of bowling alleys.

At a motel office, she could park the car out front, wedge herself in the office doorway, and keep one eye on me while she talked to the night manager. The other places were trickier. Though I sensed she didn't want to bring me into bars, sometimes she did.

In one pool room at a bowling alley, I remember the bright lights of the jukebox, the smoky haze, and the bored faces that first looked uncomfortable and then grew quiet seeing me. The smack of the pool balls at the nearest table ceased. Bowling pins tumbled in the background, and the voice of someone like Kenny Rogers or Glen Campbell streamed from the jukebox. While Mom talked to the bartender, I stared openly at a woman with glittery blue eyeshadow. She wore a leopard print blouse scattered with roses and knotted at the waist above denim shorts and black boots. Her long, skinny legs looked like the pool cue she was holding. She was tall and pretty. She also possessed qualities I couldn't yet name but today I might label as jaded or worn. I looked at Mom's back while she asked about Dad. This lady was a different kind of worn than my mother's dark, rumpled curls and her puffy winter coat.

And then there were the nights when Mom and I didn't go anywhere. Instead, uniformed police officers came to the house, taking notes in their tiny notebooks and telling us they couldn't do anything until Dad was missing for at least forty-eight hours.

The time he was gone long enough for the police to start looking for him, he finally came home on his own. That weekend, my parents and their surviving parents—Mom's dad died when she was young—holed up in my parents' bedroom. While they conferred, I passed the time making cocktails of all the flavors of soda I could find in the fridge.

For my ultimate beverage, I used one of the curvy glasses made of real glass, not plastic. The coveted vessel bore the Coca-Cola logo and a red, black, and white pattern painted like stained glass. I set out to make a rainbow of orange, root beer, and lime. When the concoction proved murky, I added ginger ale to brighten the hue. The ginger ale did nothing to enhance the color. I took a sip and then a deeper swig. The drink tasted sweet and syrupy in a way that made sarsaparilla seem mild. The bedroom door opened. Out came Grandma, Mom's mom. Had I been too noisy? Only the ginger ale bottle sat on the counter. Thankfully I'd put away the others.

"What are you doing out here?" she asked.

"Just getting some ginger ale. I was thirsty," I said. It was the first time I recall getting a glass of anything from the fridge without first asking permission. It's the only time I remember Grandma not catching me when I was getting myself into trouble.

"Don't drink too much. You'll spoil your dinner," she said. Once again, she disappeared behind the closed door.

The cocktail buzzed in my belly in an unpleasant way. I poured the rest of the drink down the sink, watching the cascade of bubbles slink down the drain. I washed and dried the glass the way I'd seen Mom do hundreds of times.

When the secret counsel concluded, I had a tummy ache, and my parents were getting divorced. No more igloos. Here we were, moving again, this time without Dad.

After a few gloomy weeks, the final day of packing arrived. Mom and I were moving in with Grandma in a neighboring town. Dad was staying behind to sell the house. A summer thunderstorm raged while Mom and I pulled my collection of dolls from around the world off their shelves. Uncle Ken gave me a Spanish flamenco dancer with a white lace mantilla. Dad's parents gave me a Hungarian doll with a bright embroidered jumper. One doll was Mom's. She got it on a trip out west with her parents when she was a kid. The doll's dress had a black print, like the shadow of a bronco rider, on a salmon background that might have been red or beige. I let the doll into my international collection because I liked the white fringe that dangled from her dress and her white cowboy boots. Plus, I was born in Panama, and the American west seemed exotic. My dolls lived the life of adventure I craved.

The last carton of our belongings sealed with tape, I hung close to Mom's hip, lest she forget me. Dad was parked on the couch in the living room, through which we had to pass on our way out. His legs stretched out before him. His hands interlocked across his thin belly. On the TV screen, NASCAR racers looped a track.

"Aren't you going to say goodbye to Angela?" Mom said. I don't recall his kiss or our embrace. What I do remember is the moment after, standing on the front porch steps. Mom rested the last cardboard box on her hip. Her green station wagon glistened in a coat of raindrops brought to life by the sun. The sight almost made up for the wood paneling I wished the car had, but the auto dealer said we couldn't afford.

"There. Do you see that?" Mom asked. My gaze followed hers skyward. A vast rainbow arced through the sky. I thought about the leprechaun on my box of Lucky Charms. Would a pot of gold be waiting for us at either end of the rainbow? We were running late to arrive at Grandma's, where she was cooking us her fried chicken, my favorite. I knew there'd be no search for a pot of gold. In the sunlight, Mom's dark hair and her warm brown eyes looked like those of my flamenco dancer. Only the doll's skin was a beautiful, warm tan, and Mom's skin was pale like mine. Tears ran down her face. I would have missed them if I wasn't studying her complexion.

"That's God's promise nothing like this will happen again," Mom said. I thought about Dad sitting on the couch, Mom and I out looking for him all those nights. Is that what she meant? I thought about the sounds I heard coming from my parents' bedroom when I lay in bed, unable to sleep. Harsh voices, Mom's sobs, other sounds I tried to decipher. Was that the dresser hitting the wall? The lamp falling? I thought about the times Dad punished me. Did she even know?

* * *

Over the next few years, while Mom and I lived with Grandma, Dad picked me up on weekends. Sometimes, he couldn't make it. Sometimes he called to cancel; other times, he didn't. When he did pick me up, he took me to his new house in a new town for the day. He taught me how to throw a fastball, a curveball, and a knuckleball, though I didn't know when I'd have occasion to play a cheap trick like a knuckleball. He taught me how to throw a football in a perfect spiral. Sometimes, he put me to work cleaning the bathroom or helping him fix up the apartment he was building on the second story. Other times, he took me hiking or fishing.

I started fishing with Dad when I was three. I'd been fishing for seven years the day we brought his canoe to a place that looked untouched by the modern world. I can't recall whether it was nearer the Delaware Water Gap or the Pine Barrens. It must have been spring. In the morning, the hot sun sent up steam on the water. Later, I could still feel the water's cool mixed with the sun's warmth. In between fishing spots, he paddled us to a shallow area so I could see the bottom of the inlet. Beneath the sparkling surface, the water was clear. Each clump of grass and each rock lay bare. Most of the rocks had rounded edges and were dark gray. The smaller stones were beige or white. One was a purply brown and more of a rectangle.

"There!" I said when Dad eased us near the rock. I stretched out my left arm, letting my waist rest against the side of the canoe, extending my legs as far as I could so I didn't tip us over.

My hand made purchase with my treasure, releasing a cloud of sand beneath the water's surface. Once seated in the canoe again, I brought my hand above my lap and stretched out my palm. The rock was unlike any I'd seen. It had carvings that looked like dandelions, though not like any dandelions I knew. After I showed Dad the prize, he explained about fossils and the Ice Age. I was holding something ancient.

As a child, I had endless energy. Fishing with Dad, I learned how to cultivate stillness. It was like the igloo all over again, but something we built together. Except for birds flying overhead and the occasional plop of a fish jumping, fishing time was quiet time. In the quiet, I could connect with my curiosity, which brought me to my fossil and gave way to a longing for the outdoor world that eventually led me to settle in Colorado. I now recognize that the natural world is waiting for us everywhere. "The world is full of magic things patiently waiting for our senses to grow sharper," wrote William Butler Yeats.

Here I am, decades since Dad and I last went fishing. Mom remarried when I was twelve. After that, Dad and his side of my family went missing from my life. Once, when I was in college at Rutgers, I tracked him down. We met at a restaurant in downtown New Brunswick. When I pressed Dad for an explanation of his absence, he said: "I thought you were better off without me." His answer burned through me like wildfire. I wanted the chance to weigh in on Dad's choice and the wisdom to know what was best. Nothing I wanted could fix the situation. I plucked a few twenties from my wallet and then slammed them on the table. I paid for both of our lunches and left an oversized tip with money I'd earned at my internship with a tech company.

Snow began to fall, the first of the season. I unlocked my bike and pedaled the short distance back to campus with fury. Wind off the Raritan River cut through my cotton jacket. Large, fluffy flakes lodged in my eyelashes. My eyes glazed with tears. I feared that I would wreck, but my legs knew the way.

One other time, after I had a near-fatal whitewater accident in mid-life, I reached out to Dad again. That time, he didn't respond. Did he even get my letter? My shame over the hurt and disappointment I expressed in my letter kept me from following up with him. If only I'd kept to Abraham Lincoln's advice on letters.

Dad died a month ago. Since then, I find myself sifting through the fragments of my childhood, trying to make sense of my father's death and his life. Some people might wonder why I'm spending so much time on a relationship that lay dormant for many years. It might be easy to conclude, as he did, that I was better off without him. Sure, I could do without his midnight roaming and his other flaws, but I needed the dad who built me igloos and took me fishing. The heart of the seven-year-old girl whose father built her a rainbow-catching igloo still beats in me.

Though the igloo melted many decades ago, his icehouse came crashing down on me again and again. Whenever I felt outdone by kids whose dads took them skiing in the Rockies, fishing in Florida, or simply grilled them hamburgers in the backyard, Dad's absence stung. That I had a loving stepfather was irrelevant. What I knew from my dad was that I didn't deserve love. In my twenties and thirties, so often when I thought I unlearned that lesson, another failed relationship said otherwise.

I find myself craving the peaceful silence of Dad's igloo. In place of that silence is one that is permanent and irreparable.

The surprise of my father's death is that where I expected to find anger over these old wounds, forgiveness blooms. And if his apology was his absence, some part of me still waits for his apology for his absence. These two conflicting desires reside together, whole.

My memory bears the only photograph I have of him that day I found the fossil. He's sitting at the bow of the canoe. In his hands, a wooden paddle rests. A bucket hat hides his receding hairline. Pale brown sideburns frame a crooked smile I'm tempted to read as a sign of contentment. When he smiles, faint lines accentuate his blue-green eyes, just like mine.

George Looney

This Alphabet of Rendered Ice

Crusted ice reflects the one street lamp
not busted out by drunks

in this city lot. Stray lines etched in snow
delineate a lexicon of ruin
as desolate & haunted as so much

of the south side of Chicago, those tenements
where the El rattles the illiterate bricks
spray-painted in flourishes of gang sign.

Once, I swore the ghost of Carl Sandburg,
hunched over, wept for the dead

& dying between tenements no one
could have lived in, though they did.

The old ghost let out a cry from his opaque lungs
as sad as anything I've ever heard.

Sad as the ice cracking off the black limbs
of oaks lining these streets. Sad as
the whine of a lone dog in this frozen air.

Sad as the futile light of the one street lamp
not busted out ghosting the ice-
crusted snow on cars in this pathetic city lot.

Sad as my breath lit by the speedometer's dim glow,
the light from the street lamp muted

through what was once just a windshield,
this alphabet of rendered ice. Sad

as wind, a music through the busted-out windows
of dilapidated tenements full of despair

& love on the south side of Chicago. Sad,
the music that ghost of a poet hummed, no
doubt remembering all it meant to be flesh.

Flying South 2021 Editors

Mary Hennessy (Poetry Editor): Mary was a registered nurse most of her adult life. She returned to school late and fell in with a community of generous, word-crazed people. Her poems have appeared in many journals and anthologies. She is a Pushcart nominee. She also serves as Poetry Editor for an online site: *Vietnam War Poetry*. Poetry is the only thing that makes sense to her anymore.

Jennifer Stevenson Vincent (Creative Non-Fiction): Jennifer was twice nominated for the Pulitzer Prize with a speciality in Civil Rights issues. She has a distinguished career in print journalism, including senior staff writer at the St. Petersburg (Fla.) Times. A founder and past President of Winston-Salem Writers, she's taught creative non-fiction at New York University, the University of South Florida and Salem College.

Bob Shar (Fiction Editor): Bob has been writing short stories for over fifty years -- reading and loving them for over sixty. His stories have appeared in *The South Carolina Review, Greensboro Review, Stoneboat, 2 Bridges Review, Bartleby Snopes, Literary Orphans* and elsewhere. He's a former factory worker, journalist, little magazine mogul (founded/edited/nearly-went-broke-running *The Crescent Review*, 1983-87), two-time Pushcart Prize nominee, retired librarian and village idiot.

Ray Morrison (Fiction Reader): Ray is an award-winning writer whose stories have appeared in numerous journals and magazines, including *Ecotone, Carve, Beloit Fiction Journal,* and *Fiction Southeast*. He is the author of the story collections, *In a World of Small Truths* (Press 53) and *I Hear the Human Noise* (Press 53). *I Hear the Human Noise* was awarded the 2020 IPPY Gold Medal for Southeast – Best Regional Fiction.

Steve Lindahl (Fiction Reader): Steve Lindahl is the author of six novels, *Motherless Soul* (ATTMP), *White Horse Regressions* (ATTMP), *Hopatcong Vision Quest* (Solstice), *Under a Warped Cross* (Solstice), *Living in a Star's Light* (Self Published) and *Chasing Margie* (Solstice). His short fiction has appeared in *The Alaska Quarterly, The Wisconsin Review, Eclipse* and others. He served for five years on the staff of *The Crescent Review.* His books can be found at http://stevelindahl.com .

Contributors

Joan Barasovska: Joan lives in Chapel Hill, NC. She cohosts a poetry series at Flyleaf Books and serves on the Board of the North Carolina Poetry Society. Joan has had poems published in *Kakalak, San Pedro River Review, Madness Muse Press, Red Fez, Speckled Trout Review,* and *Main Street Rag. Birthing Age* (Finishing Line Press, 2018) is her first book of poetry. In 2020 Joan was nominated for Best of the Net and a Pushcart Prize.

Sam Barbee: Sam's poems have appeared recently in *Poetry South, Literary Yard, Asheville Poetry Review, and Adelaide Literary Magazine,* among others; plus on-line journals *American Diversity Report, Exquisite Pandemic, Verse Virtual, The Voices Project,* and *Medusa's Kitchen.* He has a new collection, *Uncommon Book of Prayer* (2021, Main Street Rag). His previous poetry collection, *That Rain We Needed* (2016, Press 53), was a nominee for the Roanoke-Chowan Award as one of North Carolina's best poetry collections of 2016. He was awarded an "Emerging Artist's Grant" from the Winston-Salem Arts Council to publish his first collection *Changes of Venue* (Mount Olive Press); has been a featured poet on the North Carolina Public Radio Station WFDD; received the 59th Poet Laureate Award from the North Carolina Poetry Society for his poem *The Blood Watch*; and is a Pushcart nominee.

Susan Bavaria: Susan writes from Salida, Colorado. Her work has appeared in the *Bellevue Literary Review, Literary Mama, Adoptive Families Magazine* and the Georgetown University Medical School's *Interacting with the Arts* in Medicine website. Her creative nonfiction work-in-progress on adopting an older child is entitled *Cuddling the Cactus.*

Evan Benedict: Evan is a high school English teacher at Norfolk Collegiate School in Norfolk, VA. He writes poetry in his spare time, which he has because he neglects other things.

Joyce Compton Brown: Joyce has published in journals such as *Kakalak, Broadkill Review,* and *Main St. Rag*. She has won or placed in a number of contests and is the author of three chapbooks, *Bequest* (Finishing Line), *Singing with Jarred Edges* (Main St. Rag), and *Standing on the Outcrop* (Red Hawk Press). She enjoys Appalachian and social history, roots music and banjo, her husband and cat.

Les Brown: Les is professor emeritus at Gardner-Webb University. His poetry and short stories appear in journals, including *Pinesong, Kakalak,* and *Pine Mountain Sand and Gravel*. His visual art has been featured in journals including *Moonshine Review* and *Broad River Review*. Les, a 2019 Pushcart nominee, had his poetry chapbook, *A Place Where Trees Had Names*, published by Redhawk Publications in 2020.

Emily Carter: Emily is a heart and soul North Carolinian. She grew up in the Sandhills, went to Appalachian State University, and currently lives in the Southern Outer Banks town of Beaufort with her husband, John, and dog, Fergie. She has two grown children, Riley and Ryann. When she's not writing, she can be found running, cycling, paddle boarding, hiking, or enjoying most anything outdoors. Her writing inspiration comes from her family, friends, life, observations, and the overall human experience. She is a board member of The Writers' Exchange and a contributor to *Haunted Waters Press*. Her musings can be found on achicksview.com.

Mark Caskie: Mark received his MFA from UNC-Greensboro. He has recently published poetry in *StorySouth* and *The Connecticut Poetry Review*.

Kenneth Chamlee: Kenneth (Mills River, NC) is Emeritus Professor of English at Brevard College in North Carolina. His poems have appeared in *The North Carolina Literary Review, Cold Mountain Review, Ekphrasis, Worcester Review, Naugatuck River Review,* and many others, including six editions of *Kakalak: An Anthology of Carolina Poets*. He has published two award-winning chapbooks,

Absolute Faith (ByLine Press) and *Logic of the Lost* (Longleaf Press) and received three Pushcart Prize nominations. Ken recently completed a poetic biography of 19th century American landscape painter Albert Bierstadt. Check him out at www.kennethchamlee.com.

Gary Chew: Gary is an economist by profession and education at Yale University and University College London. Poetry is a new found passion during the COVID pandemic. As an emerging writer, his creative vision is to resonate with readers through heartfelt storytelling. When he is not concocting poetry, you can find this globetrotter on the road in search of fresh perspectives. Gary can be reached at contact@garychewy.com.

Sandra Dreis: Sandra is a retired Theatre Arts teacher who now writes full-time. Her debut YA novel, *Ecowarriors* received a Silver Nautilus Award in 2016. Her poems can be found in: *The Main Street Rag, Flying South, Dark Moon Lilith Press, Ravensperch, Medical Literary Messenger* and *Snapdragon*. A member of Winston Salem Writers, she lives with her beloved dogs, Bear and Darla. Sandra recently completed her first poetry chapbook, *Black Pearl Diary* edited by Tom Lombardo.

Emma Eisler: Emma is a junior English major at Cornell University with a concentration in poetry. She is Editor in Chief of the university magazine, *Kitsch*, as well as a columnist for the independent newspaper, *The Cornell Sun*. She is a recipient of the Cornell University Dorothy Sugarman Undergraduate Prize for poetry and has been published in magazines including *The Smart Set, Allegory Ridge, Cathexis Northwest Press, Prometheus Dreaming, Storm of Blue, Blackheart Magazine, SWITCHBACK,* and *Beyond Words*. She was also a semi-finalist in Digging Through the Fat's 2021 chapbook contest. Emma plans to continue pursuing a career in writing after she graduates.

Alan Elyshevitz: Alan is the author of a collection of stories, *The Widows and Orphans Fund* (SFA Press), a full-length collection of poems, *Generous Peril* (Cyberwit), and four poetry chapbooks, most recently *Mortal Hours* (SurVision). Winner of the James Hearst Poetry Prize from North American Review, he is a two-time recipient of a fellowship in fiction writing from the Pennsylvania Council on the Arts. For further information, visit https://aelyshevitz.ink.

Leigh Fairchild-Coppoletti: Leigh teaches history and lives on Martha's Vineyard. She wrote a novel about a diverse group of high school students and their mentors who find purpose and connection with each other and the natural world. While this novel and its sequel are still in development, stories (and one poem) about some of the characters can be found in *Into the Void Magazine*, *The Bangalore Review*, and *The Bread Loaf Journal*. *The Magic Box* is a sequel story about Lauren, one of the students.

Judith Ferster: Judith is a retired English professor whose post-occupation preoccupations include the environment, Palestinian rights, and monetary reform. She has published individual poems before and a volume of poetry is in preparation by Hermit Feathers Press.

Jonathan Greenhause: Winner of the Telluride Institute's 2020 Fischer Poetry Prize, his poems have recently appeared or are forthcoming in *Fourteen Hills*, *The Ginkgo Prize for Ecopoetry*, *Moon City Review*, *The New Guard*, *New York Quarterly*, and *Poetry Ireland Review*. He is currently – joyously – wearing a mask with his wife and 2 children. He is also a 3-time past contributor to *Flying South*.

Edward Hagelstein: Edward's short fiction has appeared in *Colp*, *Cowboy Jamboree*, *Black Dandy*, *Riding Light*, *Fiction Fix*, *Thuglit*, *Sterling*, *The Harbinger*, *The Fat City Review*, *Pithead Chapel*, *Sundog Lit*, *The Whistling Fire*, *Phoebe*, *Drunken Boat* and other places. He lives in Pennsylvania.

Chloe Hillary: Chloe is a writer, mum, and lawyer based in Sydney Australia. When she's not chasing a toddler with a newborn attached to her, or putting dinner on in the slow-cooker, she is reading or working on her first novel.

John J. Hohn: John resides with his wife at 2349 Walker Ave. in Winston-Salem. The city has been his hometown since 1978. He was born in Yankton, Sought Dakota, graduated with a degree in English for St. John's University (MN) in 1961. He has been writing since he was a grade school boy. Work to date includes two novels (self-published), a random poem or two in obscure quarterlies, and a blog of wide-ranging subjects, mainly non-fiction, which he has maintained off and on since 2010. He also has appeared frequently on stage over the years with local amateur theater companies. He especially enjoys open mic sessions. His acting experience has helped him with his readings. His five children are scattered across the continent. They are now middle-aged, a couple on the threshold of retirement. He also has a stepson who has been a big part of his life since he was seven years of age. John began his career as an English teacher but circumstances dictated a move into business. He worked in the financial services industry for more than forty years before retiring at the end of 2007. Since then his time has been devoted to writing and managing a small theater company.

Sharon Louise Howard: Sharon holds BA and MA degrees from the University of Central Florida. Her publishing credits include *Streetlight Magazine, Orange Blossom Review, Literally Stories, Stonecutters, Revelry, Branches, Cricket, The Formalist,* and *Shoal.*

Shannon Kawalec: Mother first, it has been Sharon's favorite choice in life. Teacher by trade, plus many other interesting experiences. Writer because she loves it (when she can find the time). She loves all genres of writing, and prefers a deadline and a challenge. Shannon believes in the power of words, that you can never travel enough, her grandmother's homemade bread, and that life is too short.

Angela La Voie: Angela's writing has been published on msnbc.com, in *CUTTHROAT 24, Blue Fifth Review: Blue Five Notebook Series, Skirt!,* and elsewhere. She holds an MFA in creative nonfiction and poetry from Antioch University Los Angeles and a B.A. in English and communication from Rutgers, The State University of New Jersey in New Brunswick. www.angelalavoie.com

George Looney: George's books include a collection of stories, *The Worst May Be Over,* which won the Elixir Press Fiction Award and was just published, *The Itinerate Circus: New and Selected Poems 1995-2020* which was also just published, the Red Mountain Press Poetry Award-winning *What Light Becomes: The Turner Variations,* the novel *Report from a Place of Burning* which was co-winner of The Leapfrog Press Fiction Award and was published in September 2018, *Hermits in Our Own Flesh: The Epistles of an Anonymous Monk* (Oloris Publishing, 2016), *Meditations Before the Windows Fail* (Lost Horse Press, 2015), the book-length poem *Structures the Wind Sings Through* (Full/Crescent Press, 2014), *Monks Beginning to Waltz* (Truman State University Press, 2012), *A Short Bestiary of Love and Madness* (Stephen F. Austin State University Press, 2011), *Open Between Us* (Turning Point, 2010), *The Precarious Rhetoric of Angels* (2005 White Pine Press Poetry Prize), *Attendant Ghosts* (Cleveland State University Press, 2000), *Animals Housed in the Pleasure of Flesh* (1995 Bluestem Award), and the *2008 Hymn of Ash* (the 2007 Elixir Press Fiction Chapbook Award). He is the founder of the BFA in Creative Writing Program at Penn State Erie, editor-in-chief of the international literary journal *Lake Effect,* translation editor of *Mid-American Review,* and co-founder of the original Chautauqua Writers' Festival.

Angela Maerea: After traveling the world for a few years, Angela discovered much about human beings and how they interact. Inspired by their stories, she moved to Paris in 2019 to pursue her master's degree in filmmaking and screenwriting to be able to share their stories with the world. When not writing or filmmaking, she enjoys hopping around Europe with her pet rabbit, Alice. Follow them both on Instagram at @iamangelamaere and @alicehopsinwonderland

Amy Marques: Amy grew up between languages and cultures, and learned, from an early age, the multiplicity of narratives. She is a collector of stories. She has penned three children's books, barely read medical papers, occasional blogs, and numerous letters. She lives in California where she writes, takes long walks, teaches at university, and tries to make a dent in her to-be-read pile. You can find her at https://amybookwhisperer.wordpress.com.

Barbara Rizza Mellin (cover artist): Barbara is a painter/printmaker from Winston-Salem, NC. As an art historian, she loves reinterpreting traditional techniques and methods for contemporary audiences. The cover image is a white-line linocut, printed by hand using non-toxic inks. The white-line technique was first introduce in the early 20th century by a group of women known as The Provincetown Printmakers, who wanted to produce multicolor prints using one block. Mellin's art has appeared in juried exhibitions throughout the US, in galleries, universities and museums and internationally online.   www.BarbaraRizzaMellin.com

Julie Means Kane: Julie is a recently retired business consultant and the grandchild of one of America's most notorious conmen. In addition to her short pieces, she is working on a history of his life that incorporates the secrets her family has kept for almost 100 years. She lived a large part of her life in rural North Carolina and is currently based in upstate New York.

Jerome Newsome: Jerome is an upcoming writer who has been published in *Aftermath Magazine, Fifty Word Stories, and Vestal Review.*

Crysta Parkinson: Crysta has always been a writer, but she took a break to raise a great big "his, hers, and ours" family. Now that there is just one left to release upon the world (complete with plans for total world domination) and she has transitioned from band-aids and book reports to long phone calls with her adult children, she is exploring her passion for writing creative non-fiction and fiction. As of 2020, she and her Kiwi hubby are transplants to Tulsa, Oklahoma. Get to know Crysta at her website: crystaparkinson.com and on Twitter @crystawrites.

Howard Pearre: Howard served in the Army from 1966 to 1969 and later with the NC National Guard. He retired after a career with NC Vocational Rehabilitation as a counselor and manager and with the Department of Veterans' Affairs as a counselor. He received an honorable mention for a short story *September, 1957* at the 2020 International Human Rights Arts Festival and is a member of Winston-Salem (NC) Writers.

Sharon Presnell: Sharon is a native North Carolinian, born and raised in Yadkin County. She received a B.S. in Biology in 1990 from NCSU and a Ph.D. in Pathology in 1995 from the Medical College of Virginia. She has worked as a scientist and organizational leader most of her career and lived in various places within the US, most recently San Diego, CA before relocating back to North Carolina in 2018. She resides in the Ardmore historic district of Winston-Salem with two Golden Retrievers, a small rescue pup, and a wonderful community of neighbors and friends. Her adult daughter lives nearby as do her parents. She loves the arts and made a promise to herself on her 50th birthday that she would give 'power and time' to her creative uprising and write (thanks, Mary Oliver).

Ramona Reeves: Ramona's fiction is forthcoming in *Bayou Magazine* and has also appeared in journals such as *New South, The Southampton Review, Ninth Letter, Pembroke Magazine,* and *Jabberwock Review*, where she won the yearly Editor's prize. Originally from

Alabama, she currently lives with her wife in Texas and serves as an associate fiction editor for *Ocotillo Review*.

Zachariah Claypole White: Zachariah lives in Chapel Hill, North Carolina, where he manages the independent bookstore Flyleaf Books. He graduated from Oberlin College in 2017, with a major in creative writing and a minor in English literature. His work has appeared in numerous publications, including *Scalawag, Sunspot Literary Journal, Toho Journal Online,* and *Sand Hills Literary Magazine*. He was longlisted for the 2020 Palette Poetry Prize. Zachariah uses writing to navigate his lifelong struggle with anxiety, depression, and OCD.

Bob Wickless: From Maryland, Bob has lived in Reidsville, North Carolina since 2008. He holds a Bachelor's in English from the University of MD and a Master's in Writing from Johns Hopkins. His poems have appeared in many magazines and literary journals— *American Scholar, Antioch Review, Poet & Critic, Poetry, Shenandoah, Southern Indiana Review,* and *Southern Poetry Review* among them. His work has also appeared in many regionally-based publications, including *Broad River Review* where he was a finalist for the Rash Award in 2020 and 2021, last year's edition of *Flying South, Iodine Poetry Journal, Kakalak 2016,17,* and *18,*and several issues of *O.Henry magazine*. He is the author of two chapbooks, *Almost Happy, (2020)* and *(Riding) Shotgun in Imaginary Cars (2021),* both from Orchard Street Press.

Carolyn Willis: Carolyn was raised in NC, has lived all over the US, and is spending her retirement in the NC foothills. She paints, eats far too much, and writes her memories to make sense of her multi-layered life.

www.ingramcontent.com/pod-product-compliance
Lightning Source LLC
Chambersburg PA
CBHW070323120726
47909CB00008B/2568